Hands-On Deep Learning for Images with TensorFlow

Build intelligent computer vision applications using
TensorFlow and Keras

Will Ballard

BIRMINGHAM - MUMBAI

Hands-On Deep Learning for Images with TensorFlow

Copyright © 2018 Packt Publishing

Commissioning Editor: Sunith Shetty
Acquisition Editor: Joshua Nadar
Content Development Editor: Dinesh Pawar
Technical Editor: Suwarna Patil
Copy Editor: SAFIS
Project Coordinator: Nidhi Joshi
Proofreader: SAFIS
Indexer: Pratik Shirodkar
Graphics: Jisha Chirayil
Production Coordinator: Shantanu Zagade

First published: July 2018

Production reference: 1300718

Published by Packt Publishing Ltd.
Livery Place
35 Livery Street
Birmingham
B3 2PB, UK.

ISBN 978-1-78953-867-0

www.packtpub.com

`mapt.io`

Mapt is an online digital library that gives you full access to over 5,000 books and videos, as well as industry leading tools to help you plan your personal development and advance your career. For more information, please visit our website.

Why subscribe?

- Spend less time learning and more time coding with practical eBooks and Videos from over 4,000 industry professionals

- Improve your learning with Skill Plans built especially for you

- Get a free eBook or video every month

- Mapt is fully searchable

- Copy and paste, print, and bookmark content

PacktPub.com

Did you know that Packt offers eBook versions of every book published, with PDF and ePub files available? You can upgrade to the eBook version at `www.PacktPub.com` and as a print book customer, you are entitled to a discount on the eBook copy. Get in touch with us at `service@packtpub.com` for more details.

At `www.PacktPub.com`, you can also read a collection of free technical articles, sign up for a range of free newsletters, and receive exclusive discounts and offers on Packt books and eBooks.

Contributors

About the author

Will Ballard is the chief technology officer at GLG, responsible for engineering and IT. He was also responsible for the design and operation of large data centers that helped run site services for customers including Gannett, Hearst Magazines, NFL.com, NPR, The Washington Post, and Whole Foods. He has also held leadership roles in software development at NetSolve (now Cisco), NetSpend, and Works.com (now Bank of America).

Packt is searching for authors like you

If you're interested in becoming an author for Packt, please visit `authors.packtpub.com` and apply today. We have worked with thousands of developers and tech professionals, just like you, to help them share their insight with the global tech community. You can make a general application, apply for a specific hot topic that we are recruiting an author for, or submit your own idea.

Table of Contents

Preface

TensorFlow is Google's popular offering for machine learning and deep learning. It has quickly become a popular choice of tool for performing fast, efficient, and accurate deep learning tasks.

This book shows you practical implementations of real-world projects, teaching you how to leverage TensorFlow's capabilities to perform efficient deep learning. In this book, you will be acquainted with the different paradigms of performing deep learning, such as deep neural nets, convolutional neural networks, recurrent neural networks, and more, and how they can be implemented using TensorFlow.

This will be demonstrated with the help of end-to-end implementations of three real-world projects on popular topic areas such as natural language processing, image classification, and fraud detection.

By the end of this book, you will have mastered all the concepts of deep learning and their implementations with TensorFlow and Keras.

Who this book is for

This book is for application developers, data scientists, and machine learning practitioners looking to integrate machine learning into application software and master deep learning by implementing practical projects in TensorFlow. Knowledge of Python programming and the basics of deep learning is required to get the most out of this book.

What this book covers

Chapter 1, *Machine Learning Toolkit*, looks into installing Docker, setting up a machine learning Docker file, sharing data back with your host computer, and running a REST service to provide the environment.

Chapter 2, *Image Data*, teaches MNIST digits, how to acquire them, how tensors are really just multidimensional arrays, and how we can encode image data and categorical or classification data as a tensor. Then, we have a quick review and a cookbook approach to consider dimensions and tensors, in order to get data prepared for machine learning.

Chapter 3, *Classical Neural Network,* covers an awful lot of material! We see the structure of the classical, or dense, neural network. We learn about activation, nonlinearity, and softmax. We then set up testing and training data and learn how to construct the network with Dropout and Flatten. We also learn all about solvers, or how machine actually learns. We then explore hyperparameters, and finally, we fine-tune our model by means of grid search.

Chapter 4, *A Convolutional Neural Network,* teaches you convolutions, which are a loosely connected way of moving over an image to extract features. Then we learn about pooling, which summarizes the most important features. We will build a convolutional neural network using these techniques and we combine many layers of convolution and pooling in order to generate a deep neural network.

Chapter 5, *An Image Classification Server,* uses a Swagger API definition to create a REST API model, which then declaratively generates the Python framework in order for us to serve that API. Then, we create a Docker container that captures not only our running code (that is, our service) but also our pre-trained machine learning model. This then forms a package so that we are able to deploy and use our container. Finally, we use this container to serve and make predictions.

To get the most out of this book

You'll need:

- Experience with command-line shell
- Experience with Python scripting or application development

Download the example code files

You can download the example code files for this book from your account at www.packtpub.com. If you purchased this book elsewhere, you can visit www.packtpub.com/support and register to have the files emailed directly to you.

You can download the code files by following these steps:

1. Log in or register at www.packtpub.com.
2. Select the **SUPPORT** tab.
3. Click on **Code Downloads & Errata**.
4. Enter the name of the book in the **Search** box and follow the onscreen instructions.

Once the file is downloaded, please make sure that you unzip or extract the folder using the latest version of:

- WinRAR/7-Zip for Windows
- Zipeg/iZip/UnRarX for Mac
- 7-Zip/PeaZip for Linux

The code bundle for the book is also hosted on GitHub at `https://github.com/PacktPublishing/Hands-On-Deep-Learning-for-Images-with-TensorFlow`. In case there's an update to the code, it will be updated on the existing GitHub repository.

We also have other code bundles from our rich catalog of books and videos available at `https://github.com/PacktPublishing/`. Check them out!

Conventions used

There are a number of text conventions used throughout this book.

`CodeInText`: Indicates code words in text, database table names, folder names, filenames, file extensions, pathnames, dummy URLs, user input, and Twitter handles. Here is an example: "You just have to type `docker --help` to make sure that everything is installed."

Any command-line input or output is written as follows:

```
C:\11519>docker build -t keras .
```

Bold: Indicates a new term, an important word, or words that you see onscreen. For example, words in menus or dialog boxes appear in the text like this. Here is an example: "We're going to select and copy the test command we'll be using later, and click on **Apply**."

 Warnings or important notes appear like this.

 Tips and tricks appear like this.

Get in touch

Feedback from our readers is always welcome.

General feedback: Email `feedback@packtpub.com` and mention the book title in the subject of your message. If you have questions about any aspect of this book, please email us at `questions@packtpub.com`.

Errata: Although we have taken every care to ensure the accuracy of our content, mistakes do happen. If you have found a mistake in this book, we would be grateful if you would report this to us. Please visit `www.packtpub.com/submit-errata`, selecting your book, clicking on the Errata Submission Form link, and entering the details.

Piracy: If you come across any illegal copies of our works in any form on the Internet, we would be grateful if you would provide us with the location address or website name. Please contact us at `copyright@packtpub.com` with a link to the material.

If you are interested in becoming an author: If there is a topic that you have expertise in and you are interested in either writing or contributing to a book, please visit `authors.packtpub.com`.

Reviews

Please leave a review. Once you have read and used this book, why not leave a review on the site that you purchased it from? Potential readers can then see and use your unbiased opinion to make purchase decisions, we at Packt can understand what you think about our products, and our authors can see your feedback on their book. Thank you!

For more information about Packt, please visit `packtpub.com`.

Machine Learning Toolkit 1

In this chapter, we're going to look at the following topics:

- Installing Docker
- Building a machine learning Docker file
- Sharing data back and forth between your host computer and your Docker container
- Building a REST service that uses the machine learning infrastructure run inside of your Docker container

Installing Docker

We'll need to download Docker to get it installed, and in this section, you'll see how we install Docker on Windows and use a script that's suitable for installation on Linux.

Let's install Docker from `https://www.docker.com/`. The quickest way to get this done is to head up to the menu. Here, we'll choose to download the version for Windows. Give it a click, which will take you right over to the Docker store, where you can download the specific installer for your platform, as shown in the following screenshot:

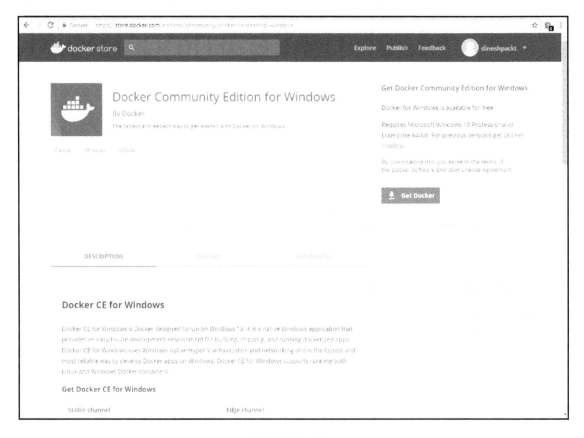

Docker installer window

All the platforms are available here. We'll just download the MSI for Windows. It downloads relatively quickly, and once it's on your PC, you can just click the MSI installer and it will quickly continue.

Installing on Ubuntu is best done with a script. So, I've provided a sample installation script (`install-docker.sh`) that will update your local package manager pointing to the official Docker distribution repositories, and then simply use apps to get the installation completed.

Getting Docker installed on Linux is pretty straightforward: you just run the `install-docker` shell script I've provided. The packages will update, download, and then install. When you get to the end of it, you just have to type `docker --help` to make sure that everything is installed:

```
⊗ ⊖ ⊚  test@test-Veriton-Series: ~
test@test-Veriton-Series:~$ docker --help

Usage:  docker [OPTIONS] COMMAND

A self-sufficient runtime for containers

Options:
      --config string      Location of client config files (default
                           "/home/test/.docker")
  -D, --debug              Enable debug mode
  -H, --host list          Daemon socket(s) to connect to
  -l, --log-level string   Set the logging level
                           ("debug"|"info"|"warn"|"error"|"fatal")
                           (default "info")
      --tls                Use TLS; implied by --tlsverify
      --tlscacert string   Trust certs signed only by this CA (default
                           "/home/test/.docker/ca.pem")
      --tlscert string     Path to TLS certificate file (default
                           "/home/test/.docker/cert.pem")
      --tlskey string      Path to TLS key file (default
                           "/home/test/.docker/key.pem")
      --tlsverify          Use TLS and verify the remote
  -v, --version            Print version information and quit
```

Output—docker --help command

Now, for GPU support, which will make your Keras and TensorFlow models run faster, there is a special version called `nvidia-docker`, which exposes devices on Ubuntu to your Docker containers to allow GPU acceleration. There's an install script for this as well (`install-nvidia-docker.sh`). Now, assuming that you do have an actual NVIDIA graphics card, you can use NVIDIA Docker in place of Docker.

Here, we're running a test command that uses the NVIDIA SMI, which is really the status program that shows you the GPU status on your machine:

```
$ sudo nvidia-docker run --rm nvidia/cuda nvidia-smi
Using default tag: latest
latest: Pulling from nvidia/cuda
e0a742c2abfd: Pull complete
486cb8339a27: Pull complete
dc6f0d824617: Pull complete
4f7a5649a30e: Pull complete
672363445ad2: Pull complete
ba1240a1e18b: Pull complete
e875cd2ab63c: Pull complete
e87b2e3b4b38: Pull complete
17f7df84dc83: Pull complete
6c05bfef6324: Pull complete
Digest: sha256:c8c492ec656ecd4472891cd01d61ed3628d195459d967f833d83ffc3770a9d80
Status: Downloaded newer image for nvidia/cuda:latest
Mon Jul 31 15:55:16 2017
+-----------------------------------------------------------------------------+
| NVIDIA-SMI 375.66                 Driver Version: 375.66                     |
|-------------------------------+----------------------+----------------------+
| GPU  Name        Persistence-M| Bus-Id        Disp.A | Volatile Uncorr. ECC |
| Fan  Temp  Perf  Pwr:Usage/Cap|         Memory-Usage | GPU-Util  Compute M. |
|===============================+======================+======================|
|   0  GeForce GTX TIT...  Off  | 0000:03:00.0     Off |                  N/A |
| 22%   44C    P8    17W / 250W  |      0MiB / 12207MiB |      0%      Default |
+-------------------------------+----------------------+----------------------+

+-----------------------------------------------------------------------------+
| Processes:                                                       GPU Memory |
|  GPU       PID   Type   Process name                             Usage      |
|=============================================================================|
|  No running processes found                                                 |
+-----------------------------------------------------------------------------+
```

GPU status

And you can see, our TITAN X is fully exposed to Docker. Getting Docker installed is a relatively easy operation.

In the next section, we're going to take a look at authoring a Docker file to set up a complete machine learning environment.

The machine learning Docker file

Now, let's dive into preparing a machine learning Docker file. In this section, we will take a look at cloning the source files, the base images that are needed for Docker, installing additional required packages, exposing a volume so that you can share your work, and exposing ports so that you'll be able to see Jupyter Notebooks, which is the tool that we'll be using to explore machine learning.

Now, you'll need to get the source code that goes with these sections. Head on over to `https://github.com/wballard/kerasvideo/tree/2018`, where you can quickly clone the repository. Here, we're just using GitHub for Windows as a relatively quick way in order to make that repository cloned, but you can use Git in any fashion you're comfortable with. It doesn't matter what directory you put these files in; we're just downloading them into our local work directory. Then, we're going to use this location as the place to begin the build of the actual Docker container.

In the clone repository, take a look at the Docker file:

```
#base image provides CUDA support on Ubuntu 16.04
FROM nvidia/cuda:9.0-cudnn7-devel

ENV CONDA_DIR /opt/conda
ENV PATH $CONDA_DIR/bin:$PATH
ENV NB_USER keras
ENV NB_UID 1000

#package updates to support conda
RUN apt-get update && \
    apt-get install -y wget git libhdf5-dev g++ graphviz

#add on conda python and make sure it is in the path
RUN mkdir -p $CONDA_DIR && \
    echo export PATH=$CONDA_DIR/bin:'$PATH' > /etc/profile.d/conda.sh && \
    wget --quiet --output-document=anaconda.sh  https://repo.anaconda.com/archive/Anaconda3-5.2.0-Linux-x86_64.sh && \
    /bin/bash /anaconda.sh -f -b -p $CONDA_DIR && \
    rm anaconda.sh
```

Docker file code

This is what we'll be using to create our environment. We're starting off with the base NVIDIA image that has the CUDA and cuDNN drivers, which will enable GPU support in the future. Now, in this next section, we're updating the package manager that will be on the container to make sure that we have `git` and `wget` updated graphics packages so that we'll be able to draw charts in our notebooks:

```
#package updates to support conda
RUN apt-get update && \
    apt-get install -y wget git libhdf5-dev g++ graphviz
```

Docker file code

Now, we're going to be installing Anaconda Python. We're downloading it from the internet, and then running it as a shell script, which will place Python on the machine. We'll clean up after we're done:

```
#add on conda python and make sure it is in the path
RUN mkdir -p $CONDA_DIR && \
    echo export PATH=$CONDA_DIR/bin:'$PATH' > /etc/profile.d/conda.sh && \
    wget --quiet --output-document=anaconda.sh  https://repo.anaconda.com/archive/Anaconda3-5.2.0-Linux-x86_64.sh && \
    /bin/bash /anaconda.sh -f -b -p $CONDA_DIR && \
    rm anaconda.sh
```

Docker file code

Anaconda is a convenient Python distribution to use for machine learning and data science tasks because it comes with pre-built math libraries, particularly Pandas, NumPy, SciPy, and scikit-learn, which are built with optimized **Intel Math Kernal Libraries**. This is because, even if you don't have a GPU, you can generally get better performance by using Anaconda. It also has the advantage of installing, not as a root or globally underneath your system, but in your home directory. Therefore, you can add it on to an existing system without worrying about breaking system components that might rely on Python, say, in the user's `bin` or whats been installed by your global package manager.

Now, we're going to be setting up a user on our container called Keras:

```
#setting up a user to run conda
RUN useradd -m -s /bin/bash -N -u $NB_UID $NB_USER && \
    mkdir -p $CONDA_DIR && \
    chown keras $CONDA_DIR -R && \
    mkdir -p /src && \
    chown keras /src
```

Docker file code

When we're running notebooks, they're going to be running as this user, so you'll know who owns the files at all times. Creating a specific user in order to set up your container isn't strictly necessary, but it is convenient to guarantee that you have a consistent setup. As you use these techniques with Docker more, you'll likely explore different base images, and those user directories set up on those images may not be exactly as you expect. For example, you may be using a different shell or have a different home directory path. Setting up your own allows this to be consistent.

Now, we're actually going to be installing conda in our environment:

```
#conda installing python, then tensorflow and keras for deep learning
RUN conda install -y python=3.6 && \
    pip install --upgrade pip && \
    pip install tensorflow==1.9.0 && \
    pip install keras==2.2.0 && \
    conda clean -yt
```

Docker file code

This will be the Python we're using here, and we'll be installing TensorFlow and Keras on top of it in order to have a complete environment. You'll notice here that we're using both conda and pip. So, conda is the package manager that comes with Anaconda Python, but you can also add packages that aren't available as conda prepackaged images by using the normal pip command. So in this fashion, you can always mix and match and get the packages you need.

In these last sections, we're setting up what's called a VOLUME:

```
#all the code samples for the video series
VOLUME ["/src"]

#serve up a jupyter notebook
USER keras
WORKDIR /src
EXPOSE 8888
CMD jupyter notebook --port=8888 --ip=0.0.0.0
```

Docker file code

This is going to allow access to the local hard drive on your machine so that your files, as you're editing them and working on them, are not lost inside the container. Then, we're exposing a port that the IPython Notebooks will be shared over. So, the container is going to be serving up port 8888, running the IPython Notebook on the container, and then you'll be able to access it directly from your PC.

Remember that these settings are from the point of view of the container: when we say VOLUME src, what we're really saying is that on the container, create a /src that's ready to receive an amount from whatever your host computer is, which we'll do in a later section when we actually run the container. Then, we say USER keras: this is the user we created before. Afterwards, we say WORKDIR, which says use the /src directory as the current working directory when we finally run our command, that is, jupyter notebook. This sets everything so that we have some reasonable defaults. We're running as the user we expect, and we're going to be in the directory that we expect as we go to run the command that's being exposed on a network port from the container from our Docker.

Now that we've prepared our Docker file, let's take a look at some security settings and how we can share data with our container.

Sharing data

In this section, we will take a look at sharing data between your Docker container and your desktop. We're going to cover some necessary security settings to allow access. We will then run the self test to make sure that we've got those security settings correct, and finally, we're going to run our actual Docker file.

Now, assuming you have Docker installed and running, you need to get into the Docker settings from the cute little whale in the **Settings...** menu. So, go to the lower right on your taskbar, right-click the whale, and select **Settings...**:

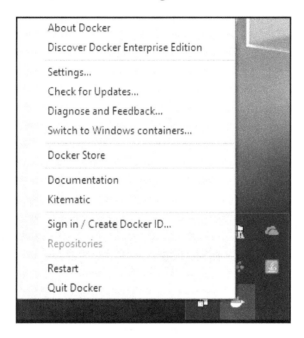

Docker Settings

There are a few security settings we need to get right in order for our VOLUME to work so that our Docker container can look at our local hard drive. I've popped this setting up from the whale, and we're going to select and copy the test command we'll be using later, and click on **Apply**:

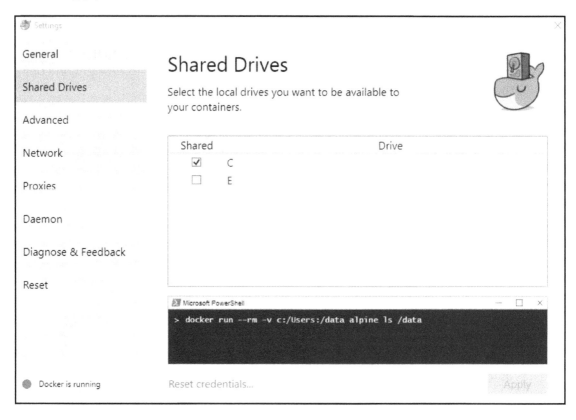

Docker Settings window

Now, this is going to pop up with a new window asking for a password so that we are allowing Docker to map a shared drive back to our PC so that our PC's hard drive is visible from within the container. This share location is where we're going to be working and editing files so that we can save our work.

Now that we have the command that we copied from the dialog, we're going to go ahead and paste it into the Command Prompt, or you can just type it in where we're going to run a test container, just to make sure that our Docker installation can actually see local hard drives:

```
C:\11519>docker run --rm -v c:/Users:/data alpine ls /data
```

So, you can see that with the -v switch, we're saying see c:/Users:, which is actually on our local PC, and then /data, which is actually on the container, which is the volume and the alpine test machine. What you can see is that it's downloading the alpine test container, and then running the ls command, and that we have access:

```
C:\11519>docker run --rm -v c:/Users:/data alpine ls /data
All Users
Default
Default User
MSSQLLaunchpad
MSSQLSERVER
MsDtsServer140
Public
SQLTELEMETRY
SSISTELEMETRY140
desktop.ini
test
```

Output— ls command

Note that if you are running on Linux, you won't have to do any of these steps; you just have to run your Docker command with sudo, depending upon which filesystem you're actually sharing. Here, we're running both docker and nvidia-docker to make sure that we have access to our home directories:

```
Command Prompt - LARGE - bash --login
wballard at horse in ~/kerasvideo on master
$ sudo docker run --rm -v /home:/data alpine ls /data
wballard
wballard at horse in ~/kerasvideo on master
$ sudo nvidia-docker run --rm -v /home:/data alpine ls /data
wballard
wballard at horse in ~/kerasvideo on master
```

Running docker and nvidia-docker

 Remember, nvidia-docker is a specialized version of Docker with plugins with a nice convenient wrapper that allows local GPU devices on your Linux installation to be visible from Docker containers. You need to remember to run it with nvidia-docker if you intend on using GPU support.

Now, we're actually going to build our container with the `docker build` command. We're going to use `-t` in order to give it a name called `keras`, and then go ahead and run the following command:

```
C:\11519>docker build -t keras .
```

This will actually run relatively quickly because I have in fact built it before on this computer, and a lot of the files are cached:

```
Step 10/14 : VOLUME ["/src"]
 ---> Running in f9bd3187c3fd
Removing intermediate container f9bd3187c3fd
 ---> d73c31db3313
Step 11/14 : USER keras
 ---> Running in e50e9a794c28
Removing intermediate container e50e9a794c28
 ---> f8495e36375f
Step 12/14 : WORKDIR /src
Removing intermediate container 0d219beb25ba
 ---> 7cfadc2f8607
Step 13/14 : EXPOSE 8888
 ---> Running in 93636868f6e7
Removing intermediate container 93636868f6e7
 ---> db4fc8b17265
Step 14/14 : CMD jupyter notebook --port=8888 --ip=0.0.0.0
 ---> Running in f4ca72a29058
Removing intermediate container f4ca72a29058
 ---> 0bc921677e4b
Successfully built 0bc921677e4b
Successfully tagged keras:latest
SECURITY WARNING: You are building a Docker image from Windows against a non-Windows Docker host. All files and directories added to build context will have
'-rwxr-xr-x' permissions. It is recommended to double check and reset permissions for sensitive files and directories.
```

Output—docker build

 Do know that, however, it can take up to 30 minutes the first time you run it.

Conveniently, the command to build on Linux is the exact same as on Windows with Docker. However, you may choose to build with `nvidia-docker` if you're working with GPU support on your Linux host. So, what does `docker build` do? Well, it takes the Docker file and executes it, downloading the packages, creating the filesystem, running commands, and then saving all of those changes against a virtual filesystem so that you can reuse that later. Every time you run the Docker container, it starts from the state you were at when you ran the build. That way, every run is consistent.

Now that we have our Docker container running, we'll move on to the next section where we'll set up and run a REST service with the Jupyter Notebook.

Machine learning REST service

Now that we've got our Docker file built and readable, we're going to run a REST service inside of our container. In this section, we will take a look at running Docker and the correct command-line arguments, the exposed URL from our REST service, and then finally we'll be verifying that Keras is fully installed and operational.

And now for the payoff: we're actually going to run our container using the docker run command. There's a couple of switches we're going to pass here. -p is going to tell us that port 8888 on the container is port 8888 on our PC, and the -v command (and we're actually going to mount our local work directory, which is where we cloned the source code from GitHub) will be mounted into the volume on the container:

```
C:\11519>docker run -p 8888:8888 -v C:/11519/:/src keras
```

Press *Enter*, and suddenly you'll be presented with a token that we're going to actually going to use to test logging in to the IPython container with our web browser:

```
C:\11519>docker run -p 8888:8888 -v C:/11519/:/src keras
[I 06:21:45.285 NotebookApp] Writing notebook server cookie secret to /home/keras/.local/share/jupyter/runtime/notebook_cookie_secret
[I 06:21:46.580 NotebookApp] JupyterLab beta preview extension loaded from /opt/conda/lib/python3.6/site-packages/jupyterlab
[I 06:21:46.580 NotebookApp] JupyterLab application directory is /opt/conda/share/jupyter/lab
[I 06:21:46.591 NotebookApp] Serving notebooks from local directory: /src
[I 06:21:46.591 NotebookApp] 0 active kernels
[I 06:21:46.591 NotebookApp] The Jupyter Notebook is running at:
[I 06:21:46.591 NotebookApp] http://986d999650b6:8888/?token=04c81b01b7c643ee2326de993d14a0b73f18b46d1733b46d
[I 06:21:46.591 NotebookApp] Use Control-C to stop this server and shut down all kernels (twice to skip confirmation).
[W 06:21:46.592 NotebookApp] No web browser found: could not locate runnable browser.
[C 06:21:46.592 NotebookApp]

    Copy/paste this URL into your browser when you connect for the first time,
    to login with a token:
        http://986d999650b6:8888/?token=04c81b01b7c643ee2326de993d14a0b73f18b46d1733b46d&token=04c81b01b7c643ee2326de993d14a0b73f18b46d1733b46d
[I 06:22:23.295 NotebookApp] 302 GET /?token=04c81b01b7c643ee2326de993d14a0b73f18b46d1733b46d&token=04c81b01b7c643ee2326de993d14a0b73f18b46d1733b46d (172.17.
0.1) 0.52ms
```

Output—docker run

Note that this token will be unique on each instance run, and will differ for your PC.

Now, if you have a GPU on a Linux-based machine, there is a separate Docker file in the `gpu` folder that you can build a Docker container with in order to get accelerated GPU support. So, as you can see here, we're just building that Docker container and calling it `keras-gpu`:

Building Docker container

It takes a little while to build the container. There's really nothing important to notice in the output; you just need to make sure that the container was actually built successfully at the end:

```
Will remove the following tarballs:

/opt/conda/pkgs
---------------
python-3.6.2-0.tar.bz2                          16.5 MB
conda-4.3.25-py36_0.tar.bz2                       510 KB
anaconda-custom-py36_0.tar.bz2                      3 KB


---------------------------------------------------------
Total:                                          17.0 MB

Removed python-3.6.2-0.tar.bz2
Removed conda-4.3.25-py36_0.tar.bz2
Removed anaconda-custom-py36_0.tar.bz2
 ---> 1a54147c0840
Removing intermediate container e0b725bd31c6
Step 10/14 : VOLUME /src
 ---> Running in 632c4299a0dd
 ---> 0e6d8e465fb3
Removing intermediate container 632c4299a0dd
Step 11/14 : USER keras
 ---> Running in b264144d3771
 ---> b6ab9c1e09e3
Removing intermediate container b264144d3771
Step 12/14 : WORKDIR /src
 ---> 7d38fa1ae4de
Removing intermediate container 563d3693946e
Step 13/14 : EXPOSE 8888
 ---> Running in 72cd863b69cd
 ---> 6fb29619c486
Removing intermediate container 72cd863b69cd
Step 14/14 : CMD jupyter notebook --port=8888 --ip=0.0.0.0
 ---> Running in bdcc3f44f7a0
 ---> 21af8fcb5c34
Removing intermediate container bdcc3f44f7a0
Successfully built 21af8fcb5c34
Successfully tagged keras-gpu:latest
```

Building Docker container

Now, with the container built, we're going to go ahead and run it. We're going to run it with `nvidia-docker`, which exposes the GPU device through to your Docker container:

```
sudo nvidia-docker run -p 8888:8888 -v ~/kerasvideo/:/src keras-gpu
```

Otherwise, the command-line switches are the same as we did for actually running the straight Keras container, except they're going to be `nvidia-docker` and `keras-gpu`. Now, once the container is up and running, you'll get a URL, and then you'll take this URL and paste it into your browser to access the IPython Notebook being served by the container:

```
wballard at horse in ~/kerasvideo on master*
$ sudo nvidia-docker run -p 8888:8888 -v ~/kerasvideo/:/src keras-gpu
[I 15:16:20.403 NotebookApp] Writing notebook server cookie secret to /home/keras/.local/share/jupyter/runtime/notebook_cookie_secret
[I 15:16:20.428 NotebookApp] Serving notebooks from local directory: /src
[I 15:16:20.428 NotebookApp] 0 active kernels
[I 15:16:20.428 NotebookApp] The Jupyter Notebook is running at: http://0.0.0.0:8888/?token=df083307dca50592659d9ca6eeb167cc35e429bd93a6b94b
[I 15:16:20.428 NotebookApp] Use Control-C to stop this server and shut down all kernels (twice to skip confirmation).
[W 15:16:20.428 NotebookApp] No web browser found: could not locate runnable browser.
[C 15:16:20.428 NotebookApp]

    Copy/paste this URL into your browser when you connect for the first time,
    to login with a token:
        http://0.0.0.0:8888/?token=df083307dca50592659d9ca6eeb167cc35e429bd93a6b94b
```

Output—docker run on Ubuntu system

Now, we'll go ahead and make a new IPython Notebook really quick. When it launches, we'll `import keras`, make sure it loads, and that takes a second in order to come up:

```
In [1]: import keras

        Using TensorFlow backend.
```

Loading Keras

Then, we'll use the following code that uses TensorFlow in order to detect GPU support:

```
from tensorflow.python.client import device_lib
print(device_lib.list_local_devices())
```

So, we'll be running the preceding bit of code in order to see the libraries and devices:

```
[name: "/cpu:0"
device_type: "CPU"
memory_limit: 268435456
locality {
}
incarnation: 14048114064309530079
, name: "/gpu:0"
device_type: "GPU"
memory_limit: 215154688
locality {
   bus_id: 1
}
incarnation: 15042970723321838406
physical_device_desc: "device: 0, name: GeForce GTX TITAN X, pci bus id: 0000:03:00.0"
]
```

Detecting libraries and devices

Now, we can see that we have GPU.

Flipping over to our web browser, go ahead and paste that URL and go:

Browser window (lacalhost)

Oops! It can't be reached because `0.0.0.0` is not a real computer; we'll switch that to `localhost`, hit *Enter*, and sure enough we have an IPython Notebook:

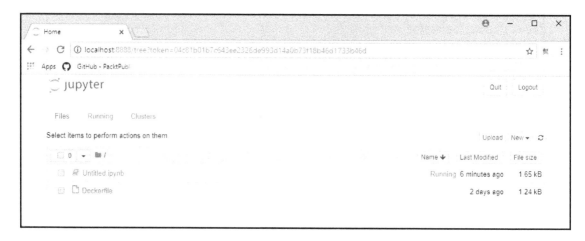

IPython Notebook

We'll go ahead and create a new Python 3 Notebook, and give it a quick test by seeing if we can import the `keras` library and make sure everything's okay.

Looks like we're all set. Our TensorFlow backend is good to go!

This is the environment that we'll be running throughout this book: a Docker container fully prepared and ready to go so that all you need to do is start it, run it, and then work with the Keras and IPython Notebooks that are hosted inside so that you can have an easy, repeatable environment every time.

Summary

In this chapter, we had a look at how to install Docker, including acquiring it from `https:/ /www.docker.com/`, setting up a machine learning Docker file, sharing data back with your host computer, and then finally, running a REST service to provide the environment we'll be using throughout this book.

In the next chapter, we're going to dive in and start looking at actual data. Then, we're going to start by understanding how to take image data and prepare it for use in machine learning models.

2
Image Data

In the previous chapter, we prepared our Machine Learning Toolkit, where we set up Keras and Docker in order to allow us to run Jupyter Notebooks to process machine learning.

In this chapter, we're going to look into preparing image data for use with machine learning and the steps that are involved in hooking that into Keras. We're going to start by learning about the MNIST digits. These are handwritten characters in the form of images that we're effectively going to perform **Optical Character Recognition (OCR)** on with machine learning. Then, we're going to talk about tensors. Tensors sounds like a math word, and it is really, but as a programmer, you've seen multidimensional arrays, so you've actually already been using tensors, and I'll show you the equivalency. Afterward, we're going to turn images into tensors. Images, as you're used to seeing them on a computer, need a special form of encoding to be used with machine learning.

Then, we're going to turn to categories; in this case, we're going to use zero through nine, which are the characters of individual digits, and turn them into category labels. Finally, we're going to recap, and I'm going to show you essentially a cookbook about how to think of data when you prepare it for machine learning.

MNIST digits

Now, let's learn about MNIST digits. In this section, we'll look at the `ImageData` notebook that I've prepared to help us understand how to deal with image data; downloading and getting the MNIST digits; looking at images as raw numbers; and then finally, visualizing the actual images based on this numeric data.

The code we're going to be working with is contained in an IPython Notebook. This is the way we've set up our container, so you're going to be running your container like we mentioned at the end of the setting up your Machine Learning Toolkit. I've also prepared an `ImageData` IPython Notebook that we're going to be working with. We will start off by importing all the necessary packages, and we're going to, turn on Matplotlib in order to automatically plot. This means that when we show an image, we don't have to call `.plot`; it'll do it for us automatically:

```
In [1]:  import keras
         import numpy as np
         import matplotlib.pyplot as plt
         %matplotlib inline

         Using TensorFlow backend.
```

Importing packages

Keras actually has the MNIST digits built-in as a dataset, so we're going to use this convenience and go ahead and load them up.

You need an internet connection because it's going to be downloading these as a file from Amazon S3.

As we load the data, there will be a Python tuple that we're going to be unpacking iPnto two sets: a **training set**, and a **testing set**:

```
In [2]:  from keras.datasets import mnist
         digits = mnist.load_data()
         (train_images, train_labels), (test_images, test_labels) = mnist.load_data()

         Images. in greyscale, are really just bytes running 0-255. Which is convenient, since Keras needs every bit of data to be numerical.
```

Python tuple

It is actually a common convention in machine learning to split your data into segments. You use it in order to see that your model is actually learning with the training set. Then, you can use a testing set to make sure that your model is not overfitting, which is really taking into consideration whether your model is memorizing the training data or whether it's actually learning.

Now, let's look at a quick setting with the format options for NumPy. As we print out arrays, we're looping through the image as an array of arrays, and then printing out the data. As you can see, the image is really just numbers from 0 to 255:

```
In [3]: np.set_printoptions(linewidth=90, formatter={'all': lambda x: '{0}'.format(x)})
        for row in train_images[0]:
            print(row)

        [0 0 0 0 0 0 0 0 0 0 0 0 0 0 0 0 0 0 0 0 0 0 0 0 0 0 0 0]
        [0 0 0 0 0 0 0 0 0 0 0 0 0 0 0 0 0 0 0 0 0 0 0 0 0 0 0 0]
        [0 0 0 0 0 0 0 0 0 0 0 0 0 0 0 0 0 0 0 0 0 0 0 0 0 0 0 0]
        [0 0 0 0 0 0 0 0 0 0 0 0 0 0 0 0 0 0 0 0 0 0 0 0 0 0 0 0]
        [0 0 0 0 0 0 0 0 0 0 0 0 0 0 0 0 0 0 0 0 0 0 0 0 0 0 0 0]
        [0 0 0 0 0 0 0 0 0 0 0 3 18 18 18 126 136 175 26 166 255 247 127 0 0 0 0]
        [0 0 0 0 0 0 0 0 30 36 94 154 170 253 253 253 253 253 225 172 253 242 195 64 0 0 0 0]
        [0 0 0 0 0 0 0 49 238 253 253 253 253 253 253 253 253 251 93 82 82 56 39 0 0 0 0 0]
        [0 0 0 0 0 0 0 18 219 253 253 253 253 253 198 182 247 241 0 0 0 0 0 0 0 0 0 0]
        [0 0 0 0 0 0 0 0 80 156 107 253 253 205 11 0 43 154 0 0 0 0 0 0 0 0 0 0]
        [0 0 0 0 0 0 0 0 0 14 1 154 253 90 0 0 0 0 0 0 0 0 0 0 0 0 0 0]
        [0 0 0 0 0 0 0 0 0 0 0 139 253 190 2 0 0 0 0 0 0 0 0 0 0 0 0 0]
        [0 0 0 0 0 0 0 0 0 0 0 11 190 253 70 0 0 0 0 0 0 0 0 0 0 0 0 0]
        [0 0 0 0 0 0 0 0 0 0 0 0 35 241 225 160 108 1 0 0 0 0 0 0 0 0 0 0]
        [0 0 0 0 0 0 0 0 0 0 0 0 0 81 240 253 253 119 25 0 0 0 0 0 0 0 0 0]
        [0 0 0 0 0 0 0 0 0 0 0 0 0 45 186 253 253 150 27 0 0 0 0 0 0 0 0 0]
        [0 0 0 0 0 0 0 0 0 0 0 0 0 0 16 93 252 253 187 0 0 0 0 0 0 0 0 0]
        [0 0 0 0 0 0 0 0 0 0 0 0 0 0 0 0 249 253 249 64 0 0 0 0 0 0 0 0]
        [0 0 0 0 0 0 0 0 0 0 0 0 0 46 130 183 253 253 207 2 0 0 0 0 0 0 0 0]
        [0 0 0 0 0 0 0 0 0 0 0 39 148 229 253 253 253 250 182 0 0 0 0 0 0 0 0 0]
        [0 0 0 0 0 0 0 0 0 24 114 221 253 253 253 253 201 78 0 0 0 0 0 0 0 0 0 0]
        [0 0 0 0 0 0 0 0 23 66 213 253 253 253 253 198 81 2 0 0 0 0 0 0 0 0 0 0]
        [0 0 0 0 0 0 18 171 219 253 253 253 253 195 80 9 0 0 0 0 0 0 0 0 0 0 0 0]
        [0 0 0 0 55 172 226 253 253 253 253 244 133 11 0 0 0 0 0 0 0 0 0 0 0 0 0 0]
        [0 0 0 0 136 253 253 253 212 135 132 16 0 0 0 0 0 0 0 0 0 0 0 0 0 0 0 0]
        [0 0 0 0 0 0 0 0 0 0 0 0 0 0 0 0 0 0 0 0 0 0 0 0 0 0 0 0]
        [0 0 0 0 0 0 0 0 0 0 0 0 0 0 0 0 0 0 0 0 0 0 0 0 0 0 0 0]
        [0 0 0 0 0 0 0 0 0 0 0 0 0 0 0 0 0 0 0 0 0 0 0 0 0 0 0 0]
```

Grey scale image (arrays of array)

This is a grayscale image, and each of these integers here records how dark that particular pixel is.

Now, let's plot the image and see what these numbers really look like. Matplotlib has a simple `plot` function that you can give an array of arrays, or basically a two-dimensional array of *XY* pixels, and it'll draw it out as an `.image` file. Following, you can see what looks an awful lot like a zero:

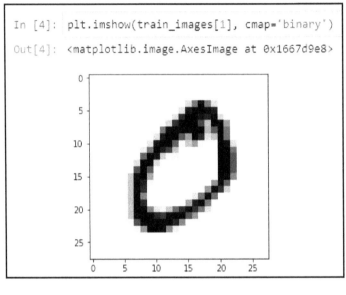

Plotting image

Tensors – multidimensional arrays

Now that we've learned a bit about MNIST digits, we're going to take the time to look at a tensor, and what a tensor is. We're going to be looking at a NumPy of multidimensional arrays. Multidimensional arrays are also called **tensors**. The math vocabulary can be mildly overwhelming, but we're going to show you that it's a lot simpler than you might think. Then, we'll look at tensor shape. Tensor shape is really the number of dimensions, or, in terms of arrays, the number of different indices that you would use to access them. And then finally, we're going to look at datatypes. The tensors, or multidimensional arrays, can hold a wide array of different datatypes, and we'll explain some of the differences.

Let's start with the basics. The most basic tensor you can imagine is a one tensor, which, in programming language is just called an array. It is just an ordered series of individual numbers packed together. Next up is a two tensor. If you look at the *Grey scale image (arrays of array)* screenshot, each row is of one dimension, and each column is another dimension.

So, row by row, this adds up to being a two tensor. Again, it's just an array of arrays. And you can see that there are trained images with the bracket zero; we're actually picking out the first image in an array of images. So, a three tensor, preceding with image data, is actually an array of images, each with an array of columns and rows of pixels. So, a three tensor is our basic way of storing black and white images.

As a quick visualization, as you can see in the image at index one, the *Xs* and the *Ys* (the coordinates that are shown following on the digit) are simply the dimensions of the tensor:

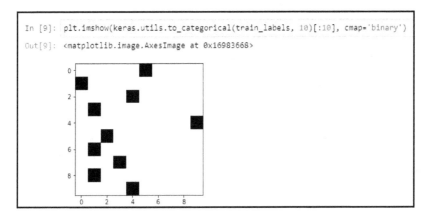

Dimension of the tensor

Now, let's talk about shape. You can see here that we call `.shape` on the NumPy multidimensional array, or tensor, and it comes back with `60000, 28, 28`:

```
In [5]: train_images.shape, train_images.dtype
Out[5]: ((60000, 28, 28), dtype('uint8'))
```

Calling .shape

These are the three dimensions that make up our three tensors. And it's just a multidimensional array. Then, there's of course the datatype, or the `dtype`, as you call it here on the NumPy multidimensional array. You can see that these images are stored as `uint8`, or 8-bit integers, to record the `0` to `255` values. Well, we'll often use this datatype for source data, particularly for black and white images like the preceding one. When we convert it into the actual machine learning format, we're going to be working with floating point.

Turning images into tensors

In the previous section, we learned a bit about what a tensor is. Now, we're going to use that knowledge to prepare image data as tensors for machine learning. First, we'll ask a question: why are we working with data in floating points? Then, we will learn the difference between samples and the data points at the end of them. Finally, we will normalize the data for use in machine learning.

So, why a floating point? Well, the real reason is that machine learning is fundamentally a math optimization problem, and when we're working with floating points, the computer is trying to optimize a series of mathematical relationships to find learned functions that can then predict outputs. So, preparing our data for machine learning does involve reformatting normal binary data, such as an image, into a series of floating point numbers, which isn't how we'd normally deal with images in terms of image processing, but it's what's required in order to get machine learning algorithms to engage.

Now, let's talk about samples. By convention, samples are always the first dimension in your multidimensional array of data. Here, we have multiple samples because machine learning fundamentally works by looking at a wide array of different data points across a wide array of different samples and then learning a function to predict outcomes based on that.

So, each image in our `train_images` multidimensional array is one of the samples we're going to be looking at. But as you can see in the *Grey scale image (arrays of array)* screenshot, the samples we have right now are definitely not in floating point; these are still in 8-bit integers.

So, we have to come up with a principled method to transform our images from 8 bit into floating point.

Now, we're going to start looking at what it really takes to prepare data for machine learning by looking at normalization. What this really means is that you take your data (in this case, it's numbers on the range of 0 to 255) and then divide it by another number so that you squash down the range from 0 to 1:

```
In [6]:  np.set_printoptions(precision=4)
         (train_images[0] / train_images.max())[5:15]

Out[6]:  array([[ 0.    ,  0.    ,  0.    ,  0.    ,  0.    ,  0.    ,  0.    ,  0.    ,  0.    ,
          0.    ,  0.    ,  0.    ,  0.0118,  0.0706,  0.0706,  0.0706,  0.4941,  0.5333,
          0.6863,  0.102 ,  0.651 ,  1.    ,  0.9686,  0.498 ,  0.    ,  0.    ,  0.    ,
          0.    ],
        [ 0.    ,  0.    ,  0.    ,  0.    ,  0.    ,  0.    ,  0.    ,  0.    ,  0.1176,
          0.1412,  0.3686,  0.6039,  0.6667,  0.9922,  0.9922,  0.9922,  0.9922,  0.9922,
          0.8824,  0.6745,  0.9922,  0.949 ,  0.7647,  0.251 ,  0.    ,  0.    ,  0.    ,
          0.    ],
        [ 0.    ,  0.    ,  0.    ,  0.    ,  0.    ,  0.    ,  0.    ,  0.1922,  0.9333,
          0.9922,  0.9922,  0.9922,  0.9922,  0.9922,  0.9922,  0.9922,  0.9922,  0.9843,
          0.3647,  0.3216,  0.3216,  0.2196,  0.1529,  0.    ,  0.    ,  0.    ,  0.    ,
          0.    ],
        [ 0.    ,  0.    ,  0.    ,  0.    ,  0.    ,  0.    ,  0.    ,  0.0706,  0.8588,
          0.9922,  0.9922,  0.9922,  0.9922,  0.9922,  0.7765,  0.7137,  0.9686,  0.9451,
          0.    ,  0.    ,  0.    ,  0.    ,  0.    ,  0.    ,  0.    ,  0.    ,  0.    ,
          0.    ],
        [ 0.    ,  0.    ,  0.    ,  0.    ,  0.    ,  0.    ,  0.    ,  0.    ,  0.3137,
          0.6118,  0.4196,  0.9922,  0.9922,  0.8039,  0.0431,  0.    ,  0.1686,  0.6039,
          0.    ,  0.    ,  0.    ,  0.    ,  0.    ,  0.    ,  0.    ,  0.    ,  0.    ,
          0.    ],
        [ 0.    ,  0.    ,  0.    ,  0.    ,  0.    ,  0.    ,  0.    ,  0.    ,  0.    ,
          0.0549,  0.0039,  0.6039,  0.9922,  0.3529,  0.    ,  0.    ,  0.    ,  0.    ,
          0.    ,  0.    ,  0.    ,  0.    ,  0.    ,  0.    ,  0.    ,  0.    ,  0.    ,
          0.    ],
        [ 0.    ,  0.    ,  0.    ,  0.    ,  0.    ,  0.    ,  0.    ,  0.    ,  0.    ,
          0.    ,  0.    ,  0.5451,  0.9922,  0.7451,  0.0078,  0.    ,  0.    ,  0.    ,
          0.    ,  0.    ,  0.    ,  0.    ,  0.    ,  0.    ,  0.    ,  0.    ,  0.    ,
          0.    ],
        [ 0.    ,  0.    ,  0.    ,  0.    ,  0.    ,  0.    ,  0.    ,  0.    ,  0.    ,
          0.    ,  0.    ,  0.0431,  0.7451,  0.9922,  0.2745,  0.    ,  0.    ,  0.    ,
          0.    ,  0.    ,  0.    ,  0.    ,  0.    ,  0.    ,  0.    ,  0.    ,  0.    ,
          0.    ],
        [ 0.    ,  0.    ,  0.    ,  0.    ,  0.    ,  0.    ,  0.    ,  0.    ,  0.    ,
          0.    ,  0.    ,  0.    ,  0.1373,  0.9451,  0.8824,  0.6275,  0.4235,  0.0039,
          0.    ,  0.    ,  0.    ,  0.    ,  0.    ,  0.    ,  0.    ,  0.    ,  0.    ,
          0.    ],
        [ 0.    ,  0.    ,  0.    ,  0.    ,  0.    ,  0.    ,  0.    ,  0.    ,  0.    ,
          0.    ,  0.    ,  0.    ,  0.    ,  0.3176,  0.9412,  0.9922,  0.9922,  0.4667,
          0.098 ,  0.    ,  0.    ,  0.    ,  0.    ,  0.    ,  0.    ,  0.    ,  0.    ,
          0.    ]])
```

Normalization output

This is needed for numerical stability in machine learning algorithms. They simply do better, converge faster, and become more accurate when your data is normalized on the range of 0 to 1.

And that's it! We've seen how to deal with input data. Two things to remember: we're going to be turning everything into floating points, and it's best if we normalize the data on the range of 0 to 1.

Turning categories into tensors

In the previous section, we looked at turning images into tensors for machine learning, and in this section, we will look at turning the output values, the categories, into tensors for machine learning.

We will cover output classes, what it means to make a discrete prediction, the concept of one-hot encoding; and then we'll visualize what one-hot encoding looks like as an image, and then we'll recap with a data preparation cookbook, which you should use to be able to deal with all kinds of image data for machine learning.

But for now, let's talk about output. When we're talking about digits, there's 0 through 9, so there's ten different classes, and not classes in the object-oriented sense, but classes in the label sense. Now, with these labels being from 0 to 9 as individual digits, the predictions we want to make need to be discrete. It won't do us any good to predict *1.5*, there's no such digit character:

```
In [7]:  train_labels[:10]

Out[7]:  array([5, 0, 4, 1, 9, 2, 1, 3, 1, 4], dtype=uint8)
```

0 to 9 predictions

So, for this, we're going to use a data transformation trick. This thing is called one-hot encoding, and it is where you take an array of label possibilities, in this case, the numbers 0 through 9, and turn them into a kind of bitmap, where each option is encoded as a column, and only one column is set to 1 (hence one-hot) for each given data sample:

```
In [8]:  keras.utils.to_categorical(train_labels, 10)[:10]

Out[8]:  array([[ 0.,  0.,  0.,  0.,  0.,  1.,  0.,  0.,  0.,  0.],
                [ 1.,  0.,  0.,  0.,  0.,  0.,  0.,  0.,  0.,  0.],
                [ 0.,  0.,  0.,  0.,  1.,  0.,  0.,  0.,  0.,  0.],
                [ 0.,  1.,  0.,  0.,  0.,  0.,  0.,  0.,  0.,  0.],
                [ 0.,  0.,  0.,  0.,  0.,  0.,  0.,  0.,  0.,  1.],
                [ 0.,  0.,  1.,  0.,  0.,  0.,  0.,  0.,  0.,  0.],
                [ 0.,  1.,  0.,  0.,  0.,  0.,  0.,  0.,  0.,  0.],
                [ 0.,  0.,  0.,  1.,  0.,  0.,  0.,  0.,  0.,  0.],
                [ 0.,  1.,  0.,  0.,  0.,  0.,  0.,  0.,  0.,  0.],
                [ 0.,  0.,  0.,  0.,  1.,  0.,  0.,  0.,  0.,  0.]])
```

One-hot encoding

Now, looking at both an input digit (here, 9), and the output bitmap, where you can see that the forth index has the ninth bit set, you can see that what we're doing in our data preparation here is having one image as an input and another image as an output. They just happen to be encoded as tensors (multidimensional arrays of floating point numbers):

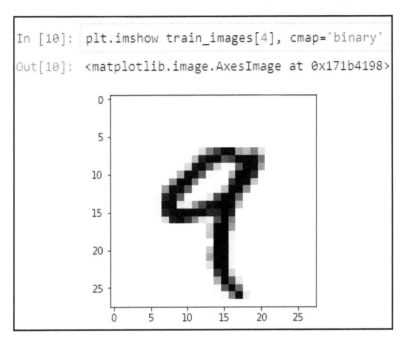

Output bitmap

What we're going to be doing when we create a machine learning algorithm is have the computer learn or discover a function that transforms the one image (the digit nine) into another image (the bitmap with one bit set on the ninth column), and that is what we mean by machine learning. Remember that tensors are just multidimensional arrays, and that the x and y values are just pixels. We normalize these values, which means we get them from the range of zero to one so that they are useful in machine learning algorithms. The labels, or output classes, are just an array of values that we're going to map, and we're going to encode these with one-hot encoding, which again means only one is hot, or set to one.

Summary

In this chapter, we learned about the MNIST digits, and how to acquire them; how tensors are really just multidimensional arrays; how we can encode image data as a tensor; how we can encode categorical or classification data as a tensor; and then we had a quick review and a cookbook approach to think about dimensions and tensors to get data prepared for machine learning.

Now that we've learned how to set up our input and output data for machine learning, we're going to move on to the next chapter, where we will create a **Classical Neural Network (CNN)**.

3
Classical Neural Network

Now that we've prepared our image data, it's time to take what we've learned and use it to build a classical, or dense neural network. In this chapter, we will cover the following topics:

- First, we'll look at classical, dense neural networks and their structure.
- Then, we'll talk about activation functions and nonlinearity.
- When we come to actually classify, we need another piece of math, `softmax`. We'll discuss why this matters later in this chapter.
- We'll look at training and testing data, as well as `Dropout` and `Flatten`, which are new network components, designed to make the networks work better.
- Then, we'll look at how machine learners actually solve.
- Finally, we'll learn about the concepts of hyperparameters and grid searches in order to fine-tune and build the best neural network that we can.

Let's get started.

Comparison between classical dense neural networks

In this section, we'll be looking at the actual structure of a classical or dense neural network. We'll start off with a sample neural network structure, and then we'll expand that to build a visualization of the network that you would need in order to understand the MNIST digits. Then, finally, we'll learn how the tensor data is actually inserted into a network.

Let's start by looking at the structure of a dense neural network. Using the network package, we will draw a picture of a neural network. The following screenshot shows the three layers that we are setting up—an input layer, an activation layer, and then an output layer—and fully connecting them:

```
In [2]:  dense = nx.Graph()
         inputs = {i: (0, i) for i in range(0, 10)}
         activations = {i+100: (1, i) for i in range(0, 10)}
         outputs= {i+1000: (2, i) for i in range(0, 2)}
         all = {**inputs, **activations, **outputs}
         #and now -- fully connected
         for input in inputs:
             for activation in activations:
                 dense.add_edge(input, activation)
         for activation in activations:
             for output in outputs:
                 dense.add_edge(activation, output)
         nx.draw_networkx_nodes(dense, all, nodelist=all.keys(), node_color='b')
         nx.draw_networkx_edges(dense, all)
         plt.axis('off')
         pass
```

Neural network with three layers

That's what these two loops in the middle are doing. They are putting an edge between every input and every activation, and then every activation and every output. That's what defines a dense neural network: the full connectivity between all inputs and all activations, and all activations and all outputs. As you can see, it generates a picture that is very densely connected, hence the name!

Now, let's expand this to two dimensions with a 28 x 28 pixel grid (that's the input network), followed by a 28 x 28 pixel activation network where the learning will take place. Ultimately, we will be landing in 10 position classification network where we'll be predicting the output digits. From the dark interconnecting lines in the following screenshot, you can see that this is a very dense structure:

```
In [3]: import itertools
        mnist = nx.Graph()
        pixels = {i: (x, y) for i, (x, y) in enumerate(itertools.product(range(0, 28), range(0, 28)))}
        activations = {i+1000: (x+30, y) for i, (x, y) in enumerate(itertools.product(range(0, 28), range(0, 28)))}
        digits = {i+2000: (70, i) for i in range(0, 10)}
        all = {**pixels, **activations, **digits}
        for pixel in pixels:
            for activation in activations:
                mnist.add_edge(pixel, activation)
        for activation in activations:
            for digit in digits:
                mnist.add_edge(activation, digit)
        nx.draw_networkx_nodes(mnist, pixels, nodelist=pixels.keys(), node_color='sienna', node_size=8)
        nx.draw_networkx_nodes(mnist, activations, nodelist=activations.keys(), node_color='skyblue', node_size=8)
        nx.draw_networkx_nodes(mnist, digits, nodelist=digits.keys(), node_color='tan', node_size=8)
        nx.draw_networkx_edges(mnist, all, width=0.1, alpha=0.5)
        plt.axis('off')
        pass
```

Two-dimensional network

In fact, it's so dense that it's actually hard to see the edges of the individual lines. These lines are where the math will be taking place inside of the network. Activation functions, which will be covered in the next section, are the math that takes place along each one of these lines. We can see from this that the relationship between the tensors and networks is relatively straightforward: The two-dimensional grid of inputs (the pixels, in the case of this image) are where the two-dimensional encoded data that we learned about in the previous section will be placed. Inside of the network, math operations (typically a dot product followed by an activation function) are the lines connecting one layer to another.

Activation and nonlinearity

We're going to be talking about why nonlinearity matters, and then we'll look at some visualizations of the two most commonly used nonlinear functions: `sigmoid` and `relu`.

So, nonlinearity may sound like a complicated mathematical concept, but all you basically need to know is that it doesn't go in a straight line. This allows neural networks to learn more complex shapes, and this learning of complex shapes inside of the structure of the network is what lets neural networks and deep learning actually learn.

So, let's take a look at the `sigmoid` function:

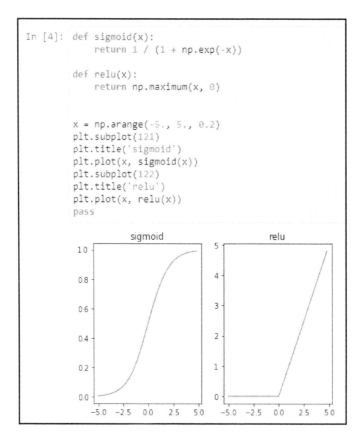

```
In [4]: def sigmoid(x):
            return 1 / (1 + np.exp(-x))

        def relu(x):
            return np.maximum(x, 0)


        x = np.arange(-5., 5., 0.2)
        plt.subplot(121)
        plt.title('sigmoid')
        plt.plot(x, sigmoid(x))
        plt.subplot(122)
        plt.title('relu')
        plt.plot(x, relu(x))
        pass
```

Sigmoid function

It's kind of an S-curve that ranges from zero to one. It's actually built out of e to an exponent and a ratio. Now, the good news is that you'll never actually have to code the math that you see here, because when we want to use `sigmoid` in Keras, we simply reference it by the name `sigmoid`.

Now, let's look at `relu`. The `relu` nonlinear function is kind of only technically a nonlinear function because when it's less than zero, it's a straight line:

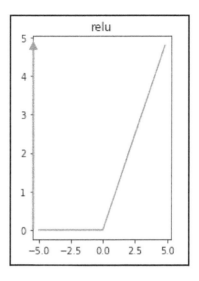

ReLu nonlinear function—less than zero

When it's greater than zero, it's also a straight line. But the combination of the two, the flat part before zero and the angle after zero together, does not form a straight line:

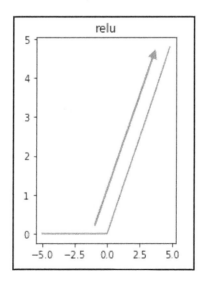

ReLu nonlinear function—greater than zero.

Because it's a very constant function, this is mathematically efficient when carried out inside of the computer, so you'll see `relu` used in many production neural network models simply because it computes faster. But the trick with `relu` functions, as we learned when we talked about normalization in the previous chapter, is that they can generate values larger than one, so various tricks and techniques in building your neural network, including normalizations and creating further layers, are often required to get `relu` functions to perform well.

A lot of what's going on in machine learning involves computing the inputs to these `relu` and `sigmoid` functions repeatedly.

 A machine learning model may have hundreds, thousands, or even millions of individual numerical parameters being run through `relu` or `sigmoid`.

There's a lot of math going on under the covers, so the interaction of a large number of nonlinearities allows a machine learner to conceptually draw a high-dimensional mathematical shape around the answers.

Softmax

In this section, we'll learn about the output activation function known as `softmax`. We'll be taking a look at how it relates to output classes, as well as learning about how `softmax` generates probability.

Let's take a look! When we're building a classifier, the neural network is going to output a stack of numbers, usually an array with one slot corresponding to each of our classes. In the case of the model we're looking at here, it's going to be digits from zero to nine. What `softmax` does is smooth out a big stack of numbers into a set of probability scores that all sum up to one:

```
In [5]: def softmax(x):
            return np.exp(x) / np.sum(np.exp(x), axis=0)
        sample_outputs = [1, 2, 5]
        softmax(sample_outputs)

Out[5]: array([ 0.01714783,  0.04661262,  0.93623955])

In [6]: softmax(sample_outputs).sum()

Out[6]: 1.0
```

Stack of numbers

This is important so that you can know which answer is the most probable. So, as an example that we can use to understand `softmax`, let's look at our array of values. We can see that there are three values. Let's assume that the neural network output is 1, 2, and 5. We're trying to classify these into red, green, and blue categories. Now, we run it through `softmax`, and we can see the probability scores. As you can clearly see here, it should be a blue, and this is expressed as a probability. The way you read out `softmax` is by using `argmax`. You look at the cell with the highest value and extract that index as your predicted class. But if you look at the actual numbers—1, 2, and 5—you can see that these add up to eight, but the output probability for 5 is 0.93. That's because `softmax` works with an exponential. It's not just a linear combination of the numbers, such as dividing five over eight and then saying 5/8 is the probability of being in that class. What we're saying here is that the strongest signals are going to dominate the weaker signals, and this exponential will actually overweigh the probability toward the class with a higher value so that your neural network is more effective in classifying when things are relatively close. Remember, with an actual neural network, you're not going to be outputting nice 1, 2, and 5 numbers—you're going to be outputting relatively small decimal numbers, such as 0.00007, really small, floating-point numbers that we then need to be able to separate out into classes.

Now you may be wondering why we should bother with this considering that you can easily tell from the numbers 1, 2, and 5 that 5 is the biggest value. Well, the idea is that if you have things expressed as probabilities, you can simulate confidence. You can, in a sense, share scores between models and know how confident your model actually is. Plus, different models will put out different numbers on different ranges. Just because you put out 1, 2, or 5 in, say, the first model you try, this doesn't mean that those have the same relative values in another model. So, crushing them down to probabilities lets you make comparisons. Now, with that math out of the way, we can start looking at building the actual neural network. The good news is you don't actually need to remember or know the math we listed just now. You just need to remember the names of the pieces of math because, in Keras, you reference activation functions with a simple name.

Training and testing data

In this section, we're going to look at pulling in training and testing data. We'll be looking at loading the actual data, then we'll revisit normalization and one-hot encoding, and then we'll have a quick discussion about why we actually use training and testing datasets.

In this section, we'll be taking what we learned in the previous chapter about preparing image data and condensing it into just a few lines of code, as shown in the following screenshot:

```
In [7]:  import keras
         from keras.datasets import mnist
         from keras.layers import Input, Dense, Dropout, Flatten
         from keras.models import Model

         Using TensorFlow backend.

In [8]:  (x_train, y_train), (x_test, y_test) = mnist.load_data()
         x_train = x_train / np.max(x_train)
         x_test = x_test / np.max(x_test)
         y_train = keras.utils.to_categorical(y_train, 10)
         y_test = keras.utils.to_categorical(y_test, 10)
```

Loading data

We load the training and testing data along with the training and testing outputs. Then, we normalize, which just means dividing by the maximum value, which we know is going to be 255. Then, we break down the output variables into categorical, or one-hot, encodings. We do these two things (normalization and one-hot encoding) in the exact same fashion for both our training and our testing datasets. It's important that our data is all prepared in the same fashion before we attempt to use it in our machine learning model. Here's a quick note about shapes. Note that the training data (both x and y) have the same initial number:

```
In [13]:  x_train.shape, y_train.shape
Out[13]:  ((60000, 28, 28), (60000, 10))
```

Loading .shape (training)

The first dimension is `60000` in both the cases, but look at the second and third dimensions (`28` and `28`)—which is the size of an input image—and the `10` figure. Well, those don't exactly have to match because what we're doing when we run this through a model is transforming the data from `28, 28` dimensions into a `10` dimension.

In addition, look at the testing data. You can see that it's `10000` in the first dimension (`28, 28`), and then `10000, 10` in the second, as shown in the following screenshot:

```
In [14]: x_test.shape, y_test.shape
Out[14]: ((10000, 28, 28), (10000, 10))
```

Loading .shape (testing)

It's really important that these dimensions match up in the appropriate fashion. So, for a training set, the first dimensions must match your `x` and `y` values (your inputs and your outputs), and on your testing set, the same thing must be true as well. But also note that the second and third dimensions, `28` and `28`, are the same for both the training and testing data, and the `10` (the output dimensions) are the same for both the testing and training data. Not getting these datasets lined up is one of the most common mistakes that is made when preparing information. But why?! In a word: **overfitting**.

Overfitting is essentially when your machine learning model memorizes a set of inputs. You can think of it as a very sophisticated hash table that has encoded the input and output mappings in a large set of numbers. But with machine learning, we don't want a hash table, even though we could easily have one. Instead, we want to have a model that can deal with unknown inputs and then predict the appropriate outputs. The testing data represents those unknown inputs. When you train your model across training data and you hold out the testing data, the testing data is there for you to validate that your machine learning model can deal with and predict data that it has never seen before.

All right, now that we've got our training and testing data loaded up, we'll move on to learning about `Dropout` and `Flatten`, and putting together an actual neural network.

Dropout and Flatten

In this section, we'll actually construct the neural network model and use `Dropout` and `Flatten` in order to create a complete neural network.

We'll start off by using the functional Keras model to actually assemble neural networks, looking at the input and layer stacks in order to assemble a neural network end to end. Then, we'll explain why we have Dropout and Flatten, and what effect they have on your model. Finally, we'll show a model summary: This is a way that you can visualize the total number of parameters and layers in a machine learning model.

Here, we're using what is known as the functional model of Keras. You can think of a neural network as a series of layers, with each one of those layers being defined by a function. The function passes a set of parameters to configure the layer, and then you hand it, as a parameter, to the previous layer in your network to chain them all together. This tiny block of code, as shown in the following screenshot, is actually a complete neural network:

```
In [9]:  input_layer = Input(shape=x_train[0].shape)
         dense_1 = Dense(32, activation='relu')(input_layer)
         dropout_1 = Dropout(0.1)(dense_1)
         dense_2 = Dense(32, activation='relu')(dropout_1)
         dropout_2 = Dropout(0.1)(dense_2)
         flat = Flatten()(dropout_2)
         output_layer = Dense(10, activation='softmax')(flat)

         model = Model(inputs=[input_layer], outputs=[output_layer])
         model.summary()
```

Functional model of Keras

We start with an input layer that's shaped in the same way as one of our input samples. In our case, we have picked one of our training images, which we know from our prior lesson has the dimensions of 28x28 pixels. Now, we pass this through a stack. A dense layer is followed by dropout_1, followed by a dense layer followed by dropout_2, which we ultimately turn into softmax activation to turn it over to the output layer. Then, we combine these together as inputs and outputs into our model. Then, we print summary, which will look like this:

```
Layer (type)                Output Shape            Param #
=================================================================
input_1 (InputLayer)        (None, 28, 28)          0
_____
dense_1 (Dense)             (None, 28, 32)          928
_____
dropout_1 (Dropout)         (None, 28, 32)          0
_____
dense_2 (Dense)             (None, 28, 32)          1056
_____
dropout_2 (Dropout)         (None, 28, 32)          0
_____
flatten_1 (Flatten)         (None, 896)             0
_____
dense_3 (Dense)             (None, 10)              8970
=================================================================
Total params: 10,954
Trainable params: 10,954
Non-trainable params: 0
_____
```

Model summary output

So, you can see from this that the parameters are passed initially to the layers, and then the layers themselves are passed to form a chain. So, what about these Dropout and Flatten layers? The Dropout parameter is essentially a trick. When we set the Dropout parameter (and here, it's 0.1) what we're telling the neural network to do is randomly disconnect 10% of the activation in each training cycle. What this does is it gets the neural network to learn to generalize; this is true learning, rather than simply memorizing the input data. The Flatten layer deals with the dimensions. Because we have a two-dimensional 28x28 pixel input image, we use Flatten to turn this into a long, single-dimensional string of numbers for 784. This gets fed to the output softmax layer.

Printing out the summary of the model is a great way to figure out the size and dimension of your parameters. This ends up being one of the trickier parts of using Keras, such as when you have a set of input samples—in our case, the 28x28 images—and you need to turn them into a single array of ten possible output values by the time you get to softmax. You can see how the shape changes as we pass it through each one of the layers. Then finally, Flatten turns it down to a single dimension for each sample, which then gets turned into a single dimension with ten possible values for the output.

All right, now it's time to run the model. Now that we understand how to put a model together, including the `Dropout` and `Flatten` layers, we'll move on to solvers, which are what we use to actually execute a machine learning model.

Solvers

In this section, we'll set up learning and optimization functions, compile the model, fit it to training and testing data, and then actually run the model and see an animation indicating the effects on loss and accuracy.

In the following screenshot, we are compiling our model with `loss`, `optimizer`, and `metrics`:

```
In [10]: model.compile(loss='categorical_crossentropy',
                       optimizer='adam',
                       metrics=['accuracy'])

         history = model.fit(x_train, y_train,
                             batch_size=64,
                             epochs=8,
                             verbose=1,
                             validation_data=(x_test, y_test))
```

Compiling model

The `loss` function is a mathematical function that tells `optimizer` how well it's doing. An `optimizer` function is a mathematical program that searches the available parameters in order to minimize the `loss` function. The `metrics` parameter are outputs from your machine learning model that should be human readable so that you can understand how well your model is running. Now, these `loss` and `optimizer` parameters are laden with math. By and large, you can approach this as a cookbook. When you are running a machine learning model with Keras, you should effectively choose `adam` (it's the default). In terms of a `loss` function, when you're working with classification problems, such as the MNIST digits, you should use categorical cross-entropy. This cookbook-type formula should serve you well.

Now, we are going to prepare to fit the model with our x training data—which consists of the actual MNIST digit images—and the y training parameter, which consists of the zero to nine categorical output labels. One new concept we have here is `batch_size`. This is the number of images per execution loop. Generally, this is limited by the available memory, but smaller batch sizes (32 to 64) generally perform better. And how about this strange word: epoch. Epochs simply refer to the number of loops. For example, when we say eight epochs, what we mean is that the machine learning model will loop over the training data eight times and will use the testing data to see how accurate the model has become eight times. As a model repeatedly looks at the same data, it improves in accuracy, as you can see in the following screenshot:

```
Train on 60000 samples, validate on 10000 samples
Epoch 1/8
60000/60000 [==============================] - 17s - loss: 0.4233 - acc: 0.8760 - val_loss: 0.2039 - val_acc: 0.9398
Epoch 2/8
60000/60000 [==============================] - 15s - loss: 0.2041 - acc: 0.9388 - val_loss: 0.1640 - val_acc: 0.9510
Epoch 3/8
60000/60000 [==============================] - 15s - loss: 0.1690 - acc: 0.9489 - val_loss: 0.1365 - val_acc: 0.9607
Epoch 4/8
60000/60000 [==============================] - 16s - loss: 0.1526 - acc: 0.9548 - val_loss: 0.1299 - val_acc: 0.9628
Epoch 5/8
60000/60000 [==============================] - 15s - loss: 0.1413 - acc: 0.9577 - val_loss: 0.1300 - val_acc: 0.9613
Epoch 6/8
60000/60000 [==============================] - 16s - loss: 0.1311 - acc: 0.9608 - val_loss: 0.1186 - val_acc: 0.9653
Epoch 7/8
60000/60000 [==============================] - 15s - loss: 0.1267 - acc: 0.9620 - val_loss: 0.1269 - val_acc: 0.9621
Epoch 8/8
60000/60000 [==============================] - 16s - loss: 0.1222 - acc: 0.9630 - val_loss: 0.1158 - val_acc: 0.9659
```

Model running

Finally, we come to the validation data, also known as the testing data. This is actually used to compute the accuracy. At the end of each epoch, the model is partially trained, and then the testing data is run through the model generating a set of trial predictions, which are used to score the accuracy. Machine learning involves an awful lot of waiting on the part of humans. We'll go ahead and skip the progress of each epoch; you'll get plenty of opportunities to watch these progress bars grow on your own when you run these samples.

Now, let's talk a little bit about the preceding output. As the progress bar grows, you can see the number of sample images it's running through. But there's also the `loss` function and the `metrics` parameter; here, we're using accuracy. So, the `loss` function that feeds back into the learner, and this is really how machine learning learns; it's trying to minimize that `loss` by iteratively setting the numerical parameters inside the model in order to get that `loss` number to go down. The accuracy is there so that you can understand what's going on. In this case, the accuracy represents how often the model guesses the right digit. So, just in terms of thinking of this as a cookbook, categorical cross-entropy is the `loss` function you effectively always want to use for a classification problem like this, and `adam` is the learning algorithm that is the most sensible default to select; `accuracy` is a great output `metrics` that you can use to see how well your model's running.

Hyperparameters

In this section, we'll explore hyperparameters, or parameters that can't quite be machine learned.

We'll also cover trainable parameters (these are the parameters that are learned by the solver), nontrainable parameters (additional parameters in the models that don't require training), and then finally, hyperparameters (parameters that aren't learned by a traditional solver).

In our *Model summary output* screenshot, pay attention to the number of trainable parameters in the highlighted section of code at the bottom of the screenshot. That is the number of individual floating-point numbers that are contained inside of our model that our `adam` optimizer, in conjunction with our categorical cross-entropy `loss` function, will be exploring in order to find the best parameter values possible. So, this trainable parameter number is the only set of numbers that is learned by our `optimizer` function. There are, however, many other numbers in this code and in the preceding screenshot. What about these nontrainable parameters? In our current model, there are zero nontrainable parameters. However, different kinds of layers in Keras may have constant values, and so they'll show up as nontrainable. Again, this simply means that there's no need for them to be trained, and that our `optimizer` function will not try to vary their values.

So, what is a hyperparameter? Well, very simply, a hyperparameter is a value—a parameter—that is outside of the model itself. So the simplest thing to think of as a hyperparameter is the actual model structure. In this case, the number of times we've created layers is a hyperparameter, the size of the layers is a hyperparameter, the `32` units we select here in our dense layers is a hyperparameter, the `0.1` dropout setting is a hyperparameter, and even the activation function itself—the choice of `relu`, say, rather than `sigmoid`—is a hyperparameter. Now you may be thinking, *wait a minute, I'm having to pick an awful lot of parameters here; I thought the machine was supposed to be learning*. It is! The trick, though, is that `optimizer` is not able to learn everything we need to know to put together an optimal model.

Grid searches

In this section, we will explore grid searches.

We'll talk a bit about optimization versus grid searching, setting up a model generator function, setting up a parameter grid and doing a grid search with cross-validation, and finally, reporting the outcomes of our grid search so we can pick the best model.

So why, fundamentally, are there two different kinds of machine learning activities here? Well, optimization solves for parameters with feedback from a `loss` function: it's highly optimized. Specifically, a solver doesn't have to try every parameter value in order to work. It uses a mathematical relationship with partial derivatives in order to move along what is called a **gradient**. This lets it go essentially downhill mathematically to find the right answer.

Grid searching isn't quite so smart. In fact, it's completely brute force. When we talk about doing a grid search, we are actually talking about exploring every possible combination of parameter values. The grid search comes from the fact that the two different sets of parameters forms a checkerboard or grid, and the grid search involves running the values that are in every square. So, as you can see, grid searching is radically less efficient than optimization. So, why would you ever even use a grid search? Well, you use it when you need to learn parameters that cannot be solved by an optimizer, which is a common scenario in machine learning. Ideally, you'd have one algorithm that solves all parameters. However, no such algorithm is currently available.

Alright, let's look at some code:

```
In [ ]: def dense_model(units, dropout):
            model = Sequential()
            model.add(Dense(units, activation='relu', input_shape=(28, 28,)))
            model.add(Dropout(dropout))
            model.add(Dense(units, activation='relu'))
            model.add(Dropout(dropout))
            model.add(Flatten())
            model.add(Dense(10, activation='softmax'))
            model.compile(loss='categorical_crossentropy',
                    optimizer='adam',
                    metrics=['accuracy'])
            return model

        hyperparameters = {
            'epochs': [1],
            'batch_size': [64],
            'units': [32, 64, 128],
            'dropout': [0.1, 0.2, 0.4]
        }

        model = KerasClassifier(build_fn=dense_model, verbose=0)
        start = time.clock()
        grid = GridSearchCV(estimator=model, param_grid=hyperparameters, cv=6, verbose=4)
        grid_result = grid.fit(x_train, y_train)
        print("Best: %f using %s" % (grid_result.best_score_, grid_result.best_params_))

        #the KerasClassifier comes back with the labels 0-9, so we use argmax
        #to turn our one-hot encoding into 0-9 digit labels
        y_true, y_pred = np.argmax(y_test, axis=1), grid.predict(x_test)
        print()
        print(classification_report(y_true, y_pred))
        print()
        print(time.clock() - start)
```

Model-generating function and conceive two hyperparameters

We're going to be using scikit-learn, a toolkit often used with Keras and other machine learning software in order to do our grid search and our classification report, which will tell us about our best model. Then, we're also going to import Keras's KerasClassifier wrapper, which makes it compatible with scikit_learn.

So now, let's focus on a model-generating function and conceive two hyperparameters. One of them will be `dropout` and the other one will be the number of units in each one of the dense hidden layers. So, we're building a function here called `dense_model` that takes `units` and `dropout` and then computes our network as we did previously. But instead of having a hard-coded `32` or `0.1` (for example), the actual parameters are going to be passed in, which is going to compile the model for us, and then return that model as an output. This time, we're using the sequential model. Previously, when we used the Keras functional model, we chained our layers together one after the other. With the sequential model, it's a lot more like a list: you start off with the sequential model and you add layer after layer, until the sequential model itself forms the chain for you. And now for the hyperparameter grid. This is where we point out some shortcomings of the grid search versus an optimizer. You can see the values we're picking in the preceding screenshot. We'll do one epoch in order to make things run faster, and we'll keep a constant `batch_size` of `64` images that will vary between `32`, `64`, and `128` hidden units, and dropouts of `0.1`, `0.2`, and `0.4`. Here's the big shortcoming of grid search: the hyperparameters you see listed here are the only ones that will be done—the grid search won't explore hyperparameter values in-between.

Now, we set up our `KerasClassifier`, handing it the model-building function we just created and setting `verbose` to `0` to hide the progress bars of each Keras run. Then, we set up a timer; I want to know how long this is going to take. Now, we set up a grid search with cross-validation. For its estimator, we give it our model, which is our `KerasClassifier` wrapper, and our `grid` parameter (see the preceding hyperparameters), and we say `cv=6`, meaning cut the data (the training data) into six different segments and then cross-validate. Train on `5`, and use one sixth to validate and iteratively repeat this in order to search for the best hyperparameter values. Also, set `verbose` to `4` so that we can see a lot of output. Now that much is running with Keras alone, we call the `fit` function going from our x training data (again, those are our input images) to our y training data (these are the labels from the digits zero to nine) and then print out our best results. Note that we haven't actually touched our testing data yet; we're going to use that in a moment to score the value of the best model reported by the grid search.

Now, we test the result. This is where we use `argmax`. Again, this is a function that looks into an array and picks out the index that has the largest value in it. Effectively, this turns an array of ten one-hot encoded values into a single number, which will be the digit that we're predicting. We then use a classification report that's going to print out x grid that shows us how often a digit was predicted correctly compared to the total number of digits that were to be predicted.

Alright, so the output of the preceding code is as follows:

```
Fitting 6 folds for each of 9 candidates, totalling 54 fits
[CV] batch_size=64, dropout=0.1, epochs=1, units=32 .................
[CV]  batch_size=64, dropout=0.1, epochs=1, units=32, score=0.9321, total=  16.7s
[CV] batch_size=64, dropout=0.1, epochs=1, units=32 .................

[Parallel(n_jobs=1)]: Done   1 out of   1 | elapsed:  21.3s remaining:    0.0s

[CV]  batch_size=64, dropout=0.1, epochs=1, units=32, score=0.9274, total=  17.3s
[CV] batch_size=64, dropout=0.1, epochs=1, units=32 .................

[Parallel(n_jobs=1)]: Done   2 out of   2 | elapsed:  43.9s remaining:    0.0s

[CV]  batch_size=64, dropout=0.1, epochs=1, units=32, score=0.9345, total=  18.2s
[CV] batch_size=64, dropout=0.1, epochs=1, units=32 .................

[Parallel(n_jobs=1)]: Done   3 out of   3 | elapsed: 1.1min remaining:    0.0s
```

Output—printing out scores

We're exploring each of the parameters in the hyperparameter grid and printing out a score. This is how the grid search searches for the best available model. When we're all done, a single model will have been picked. In this case, it's the one with the largest number of hidden units, and we're going to evaluate how well this model is using our testing data with the classification report.

In the following screenshot, you can see that the printout has each one of the digits we've recognized, as well as the precision (the percentage of time that we correctly classified the digit) and the recall (the number of the digits that we actually recalled):

```
[Parallel(n_jobs=1)]: Done  54 out of  54 | elapsed: 5.9min finished

Best: 0.952733 using {'batch_size': 64, 'dropout': 0.1, 'epochs': 1, 'units': 128}

             precision    recall  f1-score   support

          0       0.98      0.99      0.99       980
          1       0.98      0.99      0.98      1135
          2       0.96      0.93      0.94      1032
          3       0.89      0.97      0.93      1010
          4       0.95      0.97      0.96       982
          5       0.97      0.93      0.95       892
          6       0.97      0.97      0.97       958
          7       0.96      0.95      0.96      1028
          8       0.96      0.94      0.95       974
          9       0.96      0.93      0.94      1009

avg / total       0.96      0.96      0.96     10000
```

Output—final score

You can see that our score is decent: it's 96% accurate overall.

Summary

In this chapter, we actually covered an awful lot of material. We saw the structure of the classical or dense neural network. We learned about activation and nonlinearity, and we learned about `softmax`. We then set up testing and training data and we learned how to construct the network with `Dropout` and `Flatten`. We also learned all about solvers, or how machine learning actually learns. We then explored hyperparameters, and finally, we fine-tuned our model with grid search.

In the next chapter, we'll take what we've learned and alter the structure of our network to build what is called a **convolutional neural network (CNN)**.

4
A Convolutional Neural Network

In the previous chapter, we learned all about dense neural networks.

In this chapter, we're going to move on to a more recent technique: the convolutional neural network. This is an approach that you can use to process a wide array of images, and you'll find that, as we show you how it works, it's actually much more accurate and effective than the classical neural network.

In this section, we're going to learn all about convolutions and how to apply them to images, and then we're going to learn about another operation known as pooling. Armed with these two new techniques, we're going to build an actual convolutional neural network and train it in our MNIST digits, which will reveal that it's much more accurate. Finally, we're going to build an actual deep network. The idea behind deep learning is that you take these layers and combine them to make even larger networks, and we'll show you how that goes.

Convolutions

In this section, we will learn about convolutions. We're going to see the structure of a convolutional network, and then we're going to apply that to two dimensions, just like we would if we were using it for an image. Finally, we're going to discuss the benefits of a convolutional network and why you would choose to use one.

Alright, let's get started! First, we're going to import the `networkx` packages and `matplotlib`, just like we did for the classical neural network:

```
In [1]:  import numpy as np
         import matplotlib.pyplot as plt
         import networkx as nx
         import math
         %matplotlib inline
```

Importing packages

The code here is similar to what we learned in the previous chapter, but there's a minor change:

```
In [2]:  convolve = nx.Graph()
         inputs = {i: (0, i) for i in range(0, 10)}
         activations = {i+100: (1, i) for i in range(0, 10)}
         outputs= {i+1000: (2, i) for i in range(0, 2)}
         all = {**inputs, **activations, **outputs}
         #and now -- convolutionally connected

         def window(items, kernel):
             windows = []
             at = 0
             while at < len(items) + kernel:
                 windows.append(items[at:at+kernel])
                 at = at + 1
             return windows

         for i, w in enumerate(window(list(inputs.keys()), 3)):
             for input in w:
                 convolve.add_edge(input, i+100)
         for activation in activations:
             for output in outputs:
                 convolve.add_edge(activation, output)
         nx.draw_networkx_nodes(convolve, all, nodelist=all.keys(), node_color='b')
         nx.draw_networkx_edges(convolve, all)
         plt.axis('off')
         pass
```

Connecting from the inputs to the activation

You will have noticed that where we are connecting from the inputs to the activation, rather than connecting every input to every activation, we have a window. In this case, we're using a window of three, and that window then makes a sparser set of connections. The sparser set of connections, as you can see here in the actual image, means that not every input is connected to every activation; instead, there's a sliding window:

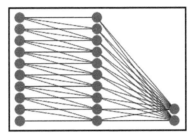

Sliding window

If you look at the lower left-hand dot, you'll see that it's actually connected one, two, three up, down to the first activation in the next column, and then similarly one, two, three up, down to the second dot in the second column. Here, we're going to visualize just a part of a network. We have a 6 x 6 grid of pixels connecting to a 6 x 6 grid of activations; so we're going to walk up the x and the y here in steps of 3. This means that this is a 3 x 3 subpatch. As you can see from the arc lines that are drawn in the output graph, what's happening is that the 3 x 3 grid and the lower left is actually being connected to one pixel on the activation on the right:

```
In [3]: import itertools
        import matplotlib.pyplot as plt
        size = 6


        mnist = nx.Graph()
        pixels = {i: (x, y) for i, (x, y) in enumerate(itertools.product(range(0, size), range(0, size)))}
        pixel_lookup = {position: i for i, position in pixels.items()}
        activations = {i+1000: (x+30, y) for i, (x, y) in enumerate(itertools.product(range(0, size), range(0, size)))}
        all = {**pixels, **activations}
        for x in range(0, 3):
            for y in range(0, 3):
                pixel = pixel_lookup[(x, y)]
                mnist.add_edge(pixel, 1000)

        nx.draw_networkx_nodes(mnist, pixels, nodelist=pixels.keys(), node_color='sienna', node_size=8)
        nx.draw_networkx_nodes(mnist, activations, nodelist=activations.keys(), node_color='skyblue', node_size=8)
        nx.draw_networkx_edges(mnist, all, alpha=0.8)
        plt.axis('off')
        pass
```

Visualizing a part of a network

The output of the preceding code is as follows:

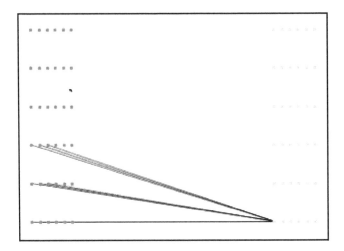

Output—visualizing a part of a network

This is different, very much so compared to the dense neural network, because it is connecting multiple inputs to a single output, as opposed to every input to every output. Using this, you can visualize how, across a larger image, this patch would slide across the image encoding regions into output variables. This has special benefits for image processing that we'll discuss now.

So, why do we do this? Regions. Convolutional neural networks encode regions of images, much like you'd think of how you look at an image with your eyes. This has important computational benefits because it groups the x and y regions of an image together computationally, creating a compact representation of the data; it's much more efficient to process a convolutional neural network because there are simply less connections to compute. Now, convolutional neural networks are not only more accurate, but they, by and large, run faster.

Pooling

Now, in this section, we'll move on to pooling. We'll be learning about the one-dimensional pooling operation; the two-dimensional pooling operation, such as you would use on an image; and then finally, we are going to discuss image channels and how they're used in this data.

Okay, from the top, we're going to be importing `keras` and some additional layers this time—particularly `MaxPooling1D`, and `MaxPooling2D`—and we're going to go ahead and import the convolutional 2D layer, which we'll be using a little bit later on. So, if you take a peek at the code, what we're doing is setting up a matrix, and this matrix just has some values. You can think of it as a square matrix of almost all ones, but I've sprinkled some higher values in here; there's 2, 3, 4, and 5. What the max pooling is going to do is extract out the highest values. So, we're going to be using a bit of a trick. To date, we've used Keras to learn machine learning models, but it turns out you can also just run the layers directly and do a little bit of math:

```
In [4]:  import keras
         from keras.datasets import mnist
         from keras.layers import Input, Dense, Dropout, Flatten, MaxPooling2D, MaxPooling1D, Conv2D
         from keras.models import Model, Sequential
         import numpy as np

         Using TensorFlow backend.
```

Importing packages

So, as you already know, you can see the values that popped into the screen; 2, 3, 4, and 5; those are actually the maximum values in the single dimension on the leading edge here:

```
In [5]:  sample = np.array([
             [1, 1, 4, 1],
             [1, 1, 1, 1],
             [2, 1, 1, 5],
             [1, 3, 1, 1],
         ])

         pool = Sequential()
         pool.add(MaxPooling1D(pool_size=(4), input_shape=(4, 4)))
         pooled = np.squeeze(pool.predict_on_batch(np.array([sample])))
         print(pooled)

         [ 2.  3.  4.  5.]
```

Max pooling operation single matrix

You can see in the preceding screenshot that the sequential model that's been put together just has the max pooling operation, and we directly insert our NumPy array into the predicted batch. We're basically skipping the training step here and just running the model as a mathematical engine. But this gives you a sense of what the max pooling operation does: it pulls out the maximum value in the dimension.

I also want to point out np.squeeze. What does this do? Well, squeeze eliminates dimensions that only have one potential value. So, remember that Keras almost always works in a batch. Here, our batch has only one batch entry: this matrix we have on the preceding screenshot. So, squeezing eliminates batch dimension so that we have a nice flat array as output.

For moving up to two dimensions, we're going to be using the MaxPooling2D operator with a pool size of 2. What this means is that we're going to be using a 2 x 2 square pool that's going to extract the maximum values. You can see from the values on the screenshot—1, 4, 3, and 5—that if you look back up at the input matrix, you'll see that the upper left-hand 1 is the maximum value of the upper left-hand region of the input, and that 4 is the maximum value of the upper right-hand region:

```
In [6]:
    pool2 = Sequential()
    pool2.add(MaxPooling2D(pool_size=(2), input_shape=(4, 4, 1)))
    pooled2 = np.squeeze(pool2.predict_on_batch(np.array([np.expand_dims(sample, -1)])))

    for row in pooled2:
        print(row)

    [ 1.  4.]
    [ 3.  5.]
```

Max pooling operation matrices

You get the basic idea! It actually took the 4 x 4 and turned it into a 2 x 2 by pulling in the maximum value. Okay, so if this is just two dimensions, why do we have three dimensions here? 4, 4, and 1. The answer is that pixels have color; they could be red, green, or blue; in which case you'd have a three in the final channel dimension. In the black and white images we're working with, you simply have a one in that dimension. So, when we pool, what we're really doing is pooling in a specific channel. In this case, we're pooling the black and white pixels together.

You can see here that there's an additional call in here, which is np.expand_dims with -1. What this does is it takes our a perfectly square array (that's 4 x 4 on the input), and adds an additional one dimension to the end to encode the channel shape so that it fits MaxPooling2D. Then, we undo that on the output with np.squeeze again, which reduces all of the one dimension axes and tosses them away, and so we get a nice square matrix on output.

Alright, so why do we carry out pooling? Well, it extracts the strong signals. What the pooling operation does is it reduces the size of the image and focuses in on the strongest values. This effectively allows the machine learner to help identify the most important pixels and regions in the image.

Building a convolutional neural network

In this section, we're going to build a full convolutional neural network. We're going to cover the MNIST digits and transform that data to have channels construct the convolutional neural network with multiple layers, and then finally, run and train our convolutional neural network and see how it compares to the classical dense network.

Alright! Let's load up our MNIST digits, as shown in the following screenshot :

```
In [7]:  (x_train, y_train), (x_test, y_test) = mnist.load_data()
         x_train = np.expand_dims(x_train / np.max(x_train), -1)
         x_test = np.expand_dims(x_test / np.max(x_test), -1)
         y_train = keras.utils.to_categorical(y_train, 10)
         y_test = keras.utils.to_categorical(y_test, 10)
```

Loading MNIST digits

You can see that we're performing a similar operation to what we did for the dense neural network, except we're making a fundamental transformation to the data. Here, we're using NumPy's `expand_dims` call (again, passing -1, meaning the last dimension) to expand our image tensors from the 28 x 28 pixel MNIST images to actually have an additional dimension of one, which encodes the color. In this case, it's a black and white image, so it's a gray scale pixel; that information is now ready to use with the convolutional layers in Keras.

Alright, let's start adding our layers. The first thing we're going to do is put together a convolutional 2D layer with a kernel size of 3 x 3. This is going to slide a 3 x 3 pixel matrix over the image, convolving that down to a smaller number of outputs, and then handing it on to a secondary convolutional 2D layer, again with a 3 x 3 matrix. This, in a sense, serves to build an image pyramid. It reduces and focuses the data in the image to an ever smaller number of dimensions, and then we pass it through the max pooling, which reduces it further still.

Now, it's starting to look like our dense neural network from before. We perform a dropout in order to avoid overfitting; we flatten it to remove all the separate dimensions so that now, there's just one dimension left; and then we pass it through a dense neural network, before finally feeding it on to our friend, softmax, who, as you remember, will classify our digits from zero to nine, the individual written digits of zero through nine. That generates our final output:

```
In [ ]:  input_shape = x_train[0].shape
         num_classes = 10
         model = Sequential()
         model.add(Conv2D(32, kernel_size=(3, 3),
                          activation='relu',
                          input_shape=input_shape))
         model.add(Conv2D(64, (3, 3), activation='relu'))
         model.add(MaxPooling2D(pool_size=(2, 2)))
         model.add(Dropout(0.25))
         model.add(Flatten())
         model.add(Dense(128, activation='relu'))
         model.add(Dropout(0.5))
         model.add(Dense(num_classes, activation='softmax'))

         model.summary()
```

Layer (type)	Output Shape	Param #
conv2d_1 (Conv2D)	(None, 26, 26, 32)	320
conv2d_2 (Conv2D)	(None, 24, 24, 64)	18496
max_pooling2d_2 (MaxPooling2	(None, 12, 12, 64)	0
dropout_1 (Dropout)	(None, 12, 12, 64)	0
flatten_1 (Flatten)	(None, 9216)	0
dense_1 (Dense)	(None, 128)	1179776
dropout_2 (Dropout)	(None, 128)	0
dense_2 (Dense)	(None, 10)	1290

```
Total params: 1,199,882
Trainable params: 1,199,882
Non-trainable params: 0
```

Performing a dropout

Alright, so this is similar to a dense network in total structure, except we've added a preprocessing set of layers that do convolution.

Alright, let's give this thing a run!

```
In [ ]: model.compile(loss='categorical_crossentropy',
                      optimizer='adam',
                      metrics=['accuracy'])

        history = model.fit(x_train, y_train,
                      batch_size=64,
                      epochs=8,
                      verbose=1,
                      validation_data=(x_test, y_test))

        Train on 60000 samples, validate on 10000 samples
        Epoch 1/8
        60000/60000 [==============================] - 193s - loss: 0.2129 - acc: 0.9342 - val_loss: 0.0523 - val_acc: 0.9823
        Epoch 2/8
        60000/60000 [==============================] - 200s - loss: 0.0793 - acc: 0.9761 - val_loss: 0.0380 - val_acc: 0.9865
        Epoch 3/8
        60000/60000 [==============================] - 206s - loss: 0.0613 - acc: 0.9813 - val_loss: 0.0345 - val_acc: 0.9894
        Epoch 4/8
        60000/60000 [==============================] - 214s - loss: 0.0504 - acc: 0.9847 - val_loss: 0.0327 - val_acc: 0.989798
        Epoch 5/8
        27008/60000 [=============>................] - ETA: 108s - loss: 0.0408 - acc: 0.9870
```

Output—preprocessing set of layers

As I mentioned previously, machine learning definitely involves human waiting, because we're going to run and train multiple layers. But you can see that the actual training code we run (the model compilation and the model fit) is the exact same as before from when we worked with the dense neural network. This is one of the benefits of Keras: the plumbing code to make it all go stays roughly the same and then you can change the architecture, putting in different layers, putting in different numbers of activations, or putting in different activation functions so that you can experiment with different network shapes that may work better with your individual set of data. In fact, you can experiment with the layer in this notebook. You can, for instance, change the activations from 32 and 64 to 64 and 128, or add in another dense layer before the final softmax output.

Now, running this training on your system, it might be time-consuming. On my machine, it took about 10 minutes to complete the entire set of training. But you'll notice right away that we're getting quite a bit better accuracy. If you cast your mind back to the last section, our dense neural network achieved an accuracy of about 96%. Our network here is a lot closer to 99%, so, by adding in convolutions, we've successfully built a much more accurate classifying neural network.

Deep neural network

Now, we're going to create an actual deep neural network using convolution.

In this section, we'll cover how to check to make sure we're running on a GPU, which is an important performance tip. Then, we'll load up our image data, and then we'll build a multiple block deep neural network, which is much deeper than anything we've created before. Finally, we'll compare the results of this deep neural network with our shallow convolutional neural network in the previous section.

Here, at the top, we're importing the necessary Python packages:

```
In [1]:  import keras
         from keras.datasets import mnist
         from keras.layers import Input, Dense, Dropout, Flatten, MaxPooling2D, MaxPooling1D, Conv2D, AlphaDropout
         from keras.models import Model, Sequential
         import numpy as np

         Using TensorFlow backend.
```

Importing packages

This is the same as we did for the standard convolutional neural network. The difference regarding making a deep neural network is that we're simply going to be using the same layers even more. In this next block, we're going directly to `tensorflow` and importing the `python` library. What is this `device_lib` we're seeing? Well, `device_lib` actually lets us list all of the devices that we have access to in order to run our neural networks. In this case, I'm running it on an nvidia-docker setup and have access to the GPU, which will boost performance:

```
In [2]:  from tensorflow.python.client import device_lib
         print(device_lib.list_local_devices())

         [name: "/cpu:0"
         device_type: "CPU"
         memory_limit: 268435456
         locality {
         }
         incarnation: 13014512740122627942
         ]
```

System status

If you don't have a GPU, that's fine! Just know that it'll take materially longer (maybe as much as 20 times longer) to run these deep neural networks on a CPU setup. Here, we're importing the MNIST digit training data, the same as before:

```
In [3]: (x_train, y_train), (x_test, y_test) = mnist.load_data()
        x_train = np.expand_dims(x_train / np.max(x_train), -1)
        x_test = np.expand_dims(x_test / np.max(x_test), -1)
        y_train = keras.utils.to_categorical(y_train, 10)
        y_test = keras.utils.to_categorical(y_test, 10)
```

Importing the MNIST digit training data

Remember that we're expanding the dimensions with the -1 (meaning that we're expanding the last dimension) to install channels, and we're normalizing this data with respect to the maximum value so that it's set up for learning the output values (the y values). Again, we switch them to categorical; there are ten different categories, each corresponding to the digits zero through nine.

Alright! Now, the thing that makes a deep neural network deep is a recurring series of layers. We say it's deep with respect to the number of layers. So, the networks we've been building previously have had one or two layers before a final output. The network we have here is going to have multiple layers arranged into blocks before a final output. Okay, looking at the first block:

```
In [*]: input_shape = x_train[0].shape
        classes = 10
        inputs = Input(shape=input_shape)
        # Block 1
        x = Conv2D(64, (3, 3), activation='relu', padding='same', name='block1_conv1')(inputs)
        x = Conv2D(64, (3, 3), activation='relu', padding='same', name='block1_conv2')(x)
        x = MaxPooling2D((2, 2), strides=(2, 2), name='block1_pool')(x)
```

Block 1

This actually forms a chain where we take a convolution of the inputs and then a convolution of that convolution, and then finally apply a max pooling in order to get the most important features. In this convolution, we're introducing a new parameter that we haven't used before: padding. In this case, we're padding it using `same` value, meaning we want the same amount of padding on all sides of the image. What this padding actually does is that when we convolve down, because of our 3 x 3 kernel size, the image ends up being, slightly smaller than the input image, so the padding places a perimeter of zeros on the edge of the image to fill in the space that we shrunk with respect to our convolution. Then, ending on the second block, you can see here that we switch from 64 activations to 128 as we attenuate the image:

```
# Block 2
x = Conv2D(128, (3, 3), activation='relu', padding='same', name='block2_conv1')(x)
x = Conv2D(128, (3, 3), activation='relu', padding='same', name='block2_conv2')(x)
x = MaxPooling2D((2, 2), strides=(2, 2), name='block2_pool')(x)
```

Block 2

Essentially, we're shrinking down the image to a denser size, so we're going from 28 pixels by 28 pixels through this pooling layer of 2 x 2 down to 14 pixels by 14 pixels, but then we're going deeper in the number of hidden layers we're using to extrapolate new features. So, you can actually think of the image honestly as a kind of pyramid, where we start with the base image and stretch it out over convolution, and narrow it down by pooling, and then stretch it out with convolution, and narrow it down by pooling, until we arrive at a shape that's just a little bit bigger than our 10 output layers. Then, we make a softmax prediction in order to generate the final outcome. Finally, in the third block, very similar to the second block, we boost up to 256 hidden features:

```
# Block 3
x = Conv2D(256, (3, 3), activation='relu', padding='same', name='block3_conv1')(x)
x = Conv2D(256, (3, 3), activation='relu', padding='same', name='block3_conv2')(x)
x = Conv2D(256, (3, 3), activation='relu', padding='same', name='block3_conv3')(x)
x = MaxPooling2D((2, 2), strides=(2, 2), name='block3_pool')(x)
```

Block 3

This is, again, stretching the image out and narrowing it down before we go to the final output classification layer where we use our good old friend, the dense neural network. We have two layers of dense encoding, which then ultimately go into a 10 output softmax.

So, you can see that a deep neural network is a combination of the convolutional neural network strung deeply together layer after layer, and then the dense neural network is used to generate the final output with softmax that we learned about in the previous sections. Let's give this thing a run!

```
Layer (type)                    Output Shape            Param #
=================================================================
input_1 (InputLayer)            (None, 28, 28, 1)        0
_____
block1_conv1 (Conv2D)           (None, 28, 28, 64)       640
_____
block1_conv2 (Conv2D)           (None, 28, 28, 64)       36928
_____
block1_pool (MaxPooling2D)      (None, 14, 14, 64)       0
_____
block2_conv1 (Conv2D)           (None, 14, 14, 128)      73856
_____
block2_conv2 (Conv2D)           (None, 14, 14, 128)      147584
_____
block2_pool (MaxPooling2D)      (None, 7, 7, 128)        0
_____
block3_conv1 (Conv2D)           (None, 7, 7, 256)        295168
_____
block3_conv2 (Conv2D)           (None, 7, 7, 256)        590080
_____
block3_conv3 (Conv2D)           (None, 7, 7, 256)        590080
_____
block3_pool (MaxPooling2D)      (None, 3, 3, 256)        0
_____
flatten (Flatten)               (None, 2304)             0
_____
fc1 (Dense)                     (None, 512)              1180160
_____
fc2 (Dense)                     (None, 512)              262656
_____
predictions (Dense)             (None, 10)               5130
=================================================================
Total params: 3,182,282
Trainable params: 3,182,282
Non-trainable params: 0
```

Output—Model summary

Okay, you can see the model summary printing out all of the layers here, chained end-to-end with 3.1 million parameters to learn. This is by far the biggest network we've created so far.

Now, it's time to train this network on our sample data and see how well it predicts. Okay, we're training the model now, and it's going relatively quickly:

```
In [*]: model.compile(loss='categorical_crossentropy',
                      optimizer='adam',
                      metrics=['accuracy'])

        history = model.fit(x_train, y_train,
                            batch_size=64,
                            epochs=8,
                            verbose=1,
                            validation_data=(x_test, y_test))

        Train on 60000 samples, validate on 10000 samples
        Epoch 1/8
        60000/60000 [==============================] - 1157s - loss: 14.4523 - acc: 0.0986 - val_loss: 14.5385 - val_acc: 0.0980
        Epoch 2/8
        60000/60000 [==============================] - 1106s - loss: 14.5270 - acc: 0.0987 - val_loss: 14.5385 - val_acc: 0.0980
        Epoch 3/8
        60000/60000 [==============================] - 1106s - loss: 14.5270 - acc: 0.0987 - val_loss: 14.5385 - val_acc: 0.0980
        Epoch 4/8
        60000/60000 [==============================] - 1136s - loss: 14.5270 - acc: 0.0987 - val_loss: 14.5385 - val_acc: 0.0980
        Epoch 5/8
        60000/60000 [==============================] - 1162s - loss: 14.5270 - acc: 0.0987 - val_loss: 14.5385 - val_acc: 0.0980
        Epoch 6/8
        23040/60000 [==========>...................] - ETA: 695s - loss: 14.5539 - acc: 0.0970
```

Training the model

On my computer, getting through the iterations took about 3.5 minutes with my Titan X GPU, which is really about as fast as you can get things to go these days with a single GPU solution. As we get to the end of the training here, you can see that we have an accuracy of 0.993, which is 1/10 or 1% better than our flat convolutional neural network. This isn't that big of an improvement it seems, but it is definitely an improvement!

So, we'll now ask: why? Simply, past 99% accuracy, marginal improvements are very, very difficult. In order to move to ever higher levels of accuracy, substantially larger networks are created, and you're going to have to spend time tuning your hyperparameters. The examples we ran in this chapter are running more than eight epochs. However, we can also change the learning rates, play with the parameters, perform a grid search, or vary the number of features. I'll leave that to you as an experiment.

Summary

Alright! We've learned about convolutions, which are a loosely connected way of moving over an image to extract features; we've learned about pooling, which summarizes the most important features; we've built a convolutional neural network using these techniques; and then finally, we combined many layers of convolution and pooling in order to generate a deep neural network.

In the next chapter, we're going to switch over to a bit more application development. We're going to be building an image classification REST server that can take different neural network models and serve those as APIs.

An Image Classification Server

5

In this chapter, we're going to be taking the machine learning models we've learned about and turn them into REST servers for image classification.

In this chapter, we'll be covering the following topics:

- Making a REST API definition with OpenAPI or Swagger
- Creating a Docker container to create a repeatable build environment
- Making predictions with our API and posting images over HTTP

REST API definition

Let's begin by defining the REST API. This is comprised of four activities: getting the project source code from GitHub with git; installing the necessary packages and reviewing the packages that will be needed in order to run our server; editing and creating the OpenAPI or Swagger definition file in YAML; and then finally handling a POST-ed image in that code that the REST API takes to turn an actual image file into a tensor.

First, we need to clone the repository that we've provided in order to have a REST service. I'm getting this over HTTPS and cloning it with the command line:

```
$ git clone https://github.com/wballard/kerasvideo-server/tree/2018.git
```

You can put it in any directory you like. Afterwards, we'll be able to use this source code for the rest of this section, and in the remaining chapters of this book:

```
test@test:~/Desktop/11519/kerasvideo-server-2018$ ls
Dockerfile   mnist.py      readme.md                   var
Makefile     models.yaml   requirements.txt  train_mnist.py
```

Files in Kerasvideo-server-2018

Using my locally installed Python, I'm actually using `pip` here to install the requirements for this service:

```
$ pip install -r requirements.txt
```

Installing them into the Python that we're working with will allow us to run the service locally in debug mode. However, if you're just going to review the source code and run and build the Docker container, which we'll get to later on, there's no need to do this step.

Let's open up our `models.yaml` file:

```yaml
swagger: "2.0"

info:
  title: Keras Model Server
  version: "1.0"

paths:
  /mnist/classify:
    post:
      summary: Classify Digits
      description: Generates a greeting message from a post, such as curl -F file=@sample.png
http://localhost:5000/mnist/classify
      operationId: mnist.post_image
      consumes:
        - multipart/form-data
      produces:
        - text/json;
      responses:
        200:
          description: classification response
          schema:
            type: string
          examples:
            "text/json": "{digit: 0}"
      parameters:
        - name: file
          in: formData
          description: Image file to classify as a digit.
          required: true
          type: file
```

The Models.yaml file

This YAML file is a Swagger API definition, also known as an OpenAPI. Inside this file, the API is defined declaratively; we specify the endpoints, the configurations, the parameters, the return codes, and additional comments that serve as runtime documentation. At the head of the file here, we specify that it's Swagger 2.0, which is the most commonly used version of OpenAPI today. Then, immediately thereafter, we have an information block, which really just describes the name of our API and serves as the version number and title; this is just descriptive metadata about our API. The bulk of the configuration is concerned with paths. You can see from the preceding screenshot that we have /mnist/classify. This is actually our main API endpoint and definition. We specify that it takes a post; we have the summary description and operation ID. The operation ID (mnist.post_image) is what ties into our code in the framework when we actually launch it. If you look at this closer, you can see that it consumes multipart/form data, meaning that we're actually going to be posting a file to this API endpoint, much like you would upload a file with an HTML form. Finally, this is going to return JSON with a 200 result code. The interesting thing about this definition is that we're almost done with our server. By declaring the API with YAML, we then marry this up with a very small amount of code, using the connection framework to provide a REST API.

Let's take a look! We're going to open up our server.py:

```
"""
This is the server module to create a `connexion` application. Run it from the
command line with python for testing.abs

The application is named to be compatible with uwsgi.
"""

import os

import connexion

PORT = int(os.environ.get('PORT', 5000))

application = connexion.App(__name__, port=PORT, specification_dir='')
application.add_api('models.yaml')


if __name__ == '__main__':
    application.run(server='tornado', debug=True)
```

The server.py file

This is the actual code we're going to use to serve the YAML configuration we just made as a REST server. As you can see, there's very little to it. We specify a port, we create a connection application using that name and port, and we add an API with `models.yaml`. This is probably the most minimal web server or REST server you'll have ever created because the connection framework is using that YAML definition that we just created to dynamically create the REST endpoints and then map through to a final piece of code, which actually serves.

Let's take a look at that now:

```
"""
This module serves as the API provider for MNIST digit processing.
"""

import io
import json

import numpy as np
from keras.models import load_model
from PIL import Image
from PIL.ImageOps import fit, grayscale

MNIST_MODEL = load_model('var/data/mnist.h5')
print(MNIST_MODEL.summary())

def post_image(file):
    """
    Given a posted image, classify it using the pretrained model.

    This will take 'any size' image, and scale it down to 28x28 like our MNIST
    training data -- and convert to grayscale.

    Parameters
    ----------
```

The mnist.py file

This final piece of code is our MNIST module. If you remember YAML, we had `mnist.post_image`, which means the module MNIST, and the function `post_image`. You can see in the preceding `mnist.py` file that we're importing a few pieces of code, namely the `PIL`, which is the image library we'll be using to process images. From here, we're going to be preloading the `MNIST_MODEL`. This is a module-level variable containing the trained machine learning model; we'll take a look at that model in the next section. Now, it's the job of this `post_image` method to take a file, which is a posted file via an HTML multipart form, take it as bytes (where you can see we have `file.read`), and turn it into an image with `Image.open`:

```
#using Pillow -- python image processing -- to turn the poseted file into bytes
image = Image.open(io.BytesIO(file.read()))
image = grayscale(fit(image, (28, 28)))
image_bytes = image.tobytes()
#image needs to be a 'batch' though only of one, and with one channel -- grayscale
image_array = np.reshape(np.frombuffer(image_bytes, dtype=np.uint8), (1, 28, 28, 1))
prediction = MNIST_MODEL.predict(image_array)
#argmax to reverse the one hot encoding
digit = np.argmax(prediction[0])
#need to convert to int -- numpy.int64 isn't known to serialize
return json.dumps({'digit': int(digit)})
```

Using the Pillow command

This actually takes the bytes stream of the uploaded file and turns it into an image object in memory. Because we've trained the MNIST_MODEL on the standard size images of 28 x 28, we have to resize the image (just in case you've posted one that's larger than we're used to) and then turn it grayscale (again, in case you posted a color image). So, we're normalizing the data here to match the expectations of the MNIST_MODEL. With that in hand, we're going to resize it. We are going to resize this image using the things we've learned about creating samples and batches. So, the first dimension is 1, which is the sample (again, only one image in this sample that we're posting); 28 x 28 is the size; and then we have 1, which is the number of channels (here, it's just the grayscale). We take this set of data and predict it. This is going to return an array of numbers, which are the 0 through 9 one-hot encodings. We also have to reverse the one-hot encoding, which is the role of argmax. If you recall, it's a batch of 1, so we pick off the 0 with the element of the returned array to match up with our input, and then use argmax in order to find which digit we've been classified as (again, reversing the one-hot encoding). Finally, we return this as a bit of JSON code.

 The JSON encoder doesn't understand NumPy integer types, so we just do a quick cast down to a Python integer.

Now that we understand how to make a REST service with connections and hook into the Keras model, let's take a look at turning this into a Docker container so that we can have a recreatable, deployable runtime environment.

Trained models in Docker containers

In the last section, we looked at creating a REST server for classifying images. In this section, we're going to look at preparing a Docker container to create a reasonable runtime environment for that server. As we look into this, we're going to ask the question: *why use Docker to package up our machine learning models?* Then, we'll actually investigate model training and then save a trained model for use in the Docker container followed by our server Dockerfile, which will package this all together. Finally, we'll build the Docker container for the reusable runtime of our REST service.

So, why Docker? Fundamentally, it makes your trained model portable. Unlike most of the programs you've created, which are mostly code with a separate database, a machine learning model is typically going to have a relatively large set of files that are the stored learned networks. These files are often too large to check into GitHub or to deploy by other convenient means. While some folks will publish them on S3 or other file-sharing solutions, packaging up your code for the runtime of your REST service along with your trained model, in my opinion, provides a great way to create a portable runtime environment that you can use across multiple different cloud providers, including Amazon, Microsoft, and Kubernetes.

Now, let's take a look at our `train_mnist` Python source file. This is a script that you simply run from the command line. It will train a Keras model in order to predict MNIST digits. This is very similar to what we've done in previous sections, and, as you can see in the following screenshot, we import all the necessary layers for our Keras model and then print out look at our local devices:

```
"""
Train an MNIST image recognition model.
"""

import keras
import numpy as np
from keras.datasets import mnist
from keras.layers import (Conv2D, Dense, Dropout, Flatten, Input, MaxPooling1D,
                          MaxPooling2D, BatchNormalization)
from keras.models import Model, Sequential
from tensorflow.python.client import device_lib

print(device_lib.list_local_devices())
```

The train_minst file

Then, we load up the training and testing data, as we did in the previous sections, and we pull this data in from Keras's prepackaged MNIST digits and models. Finally, we convert it into categorical data (again, with one-hot encoding) in order to predict digits:

```python
# training data
(x_train, y_train), (x_test, y_test) = mnist.load_data()
x_train = np.expand_dims(x_train / np.max(x_train), -1)
x_test = np.expand_dims(x_test / np.max(x_test), -1)
y_train = keras.utils.to_categorical(y_train, 10)
y_test = keras.utils.to_categorical(y_test, 10)
```

Training data

The model we'll be training in order to package up here is a relatively straightforward convolutional model, similar to what we explored in previous chapters:

```python
# our convolutional model
input_shape = x_train[0].shape
num_classes = 10
model = Sequential()
model.add(Conv2D(32, kernel_size=(3, 3),
                 activation='relu',
                 input_shape=input_shape))
model.add(Conv2D(64, (3, 3), activation='relu'))
model.add(MaxPooling2D(pool_size=(2, 2)))
model.add(Dropout(0.25))
model.add(Flatten())
model.add(Dense(128, activation='relu'))
model.add(Dropout(0.5))
model.add(Dense(num_classes, activation='softmax'))
print(model.summary())

model.compile(loss='categorical_crossentropy',
              optimizer='adam',
              metrics=['accuracy'])
history = model.fit(x_train, y_train,
                    batch_size=64,
                    epochs=8,
                    verbose=1,
                    validation_data=(x_test, y_test))
```

Convolutional model

We're using sequential to have an `input_shape` down to ten classes and two series of convolutions to build features. We'll use max pooling in order to reduce this, dropout in order to prevent overfitting, and then flatten it out to the final output with 128 layer activations so that we can then do another dropout. Finally, we will perform dense encoding with softmax. Remember, softmax is the way we convert the final scores into a set of probabilities across each of the classes.

Then, we'll use something that we haven't used before, which is `model.save`:

```
# save the model in an HDF5 file, built in to keras
model.save('var/data/mnist.h5')
```

Save the model in an HDF5 file

We're actually going to save the entire pretrained model after we go through fitting with the learning algorithm in order to have an `.h5` file, which is really a set of matrix definitions, the actual values that we learned, as well as the shape of the overall network, so that we can load this up and reuse our training network. Regarding this training script, we're going to be using it inside of a Dockerfile so that we can create a Docker container with a pre-trained and saved model stored in the Docker image.

Here, we're taking a look at the Docker file:

```
#base image provides CUDA support on Ubuntu 16.04
FROM nvidia/cuda:9.0-cudnn7-devel

ENV CONDA_DIR /opt/conda
ENV PATH $CONDA_DIR/bin:$PATH
ENV NB_USER keras
ENV NB_UID 1000

#package updates to support conda
RUN apt-get update && \
    apt-get install -y wget git libhdf5-dev g++ graphviz

#add on conda python and make sure it is in the path
RUN mkdir -p $CONDA_DIR && \
    echo export PATH=$CONDA_DIR/bin:'$PATH' > /etc/profile.d/conda.sh && \
    wget --quiet --output-document=miniconda.sh https://repo.continuum.io/miniconda/Miniconda3-
latest-Linux-x86_64.sh && \
    /bin/bash /miniconda.sh -f -b -p $CONDA_DIR && \
    rm miniconda.sh

#setting up a user to run conda
RUN useradd -m -s /bin/bash -N -u $NB_UID $NB_USER && \
    mkdir -p $CONDA_DIR && \
    chown keras $CONDA_DIR -R && \
    mkdir -p /src && \
    chown keras /src
```

The Docker file

This is where we're going to utilize our training script and package up a reusable container. We're starting from the same NVIDIA image we used before when we prepared a Dockerfile, and we'll be installing a few packages that are necessary for full support at the Python Miniconda. But the big difference here is that, instead of using Anaconda, which is the full distribution with many packages, we're using Miniconda, which is a stripped down, highly portable distribution of Python on top of which we will only then install the necessary packages. Now that we've got Miniconda installed, we're going to create a user to run this Keras and then copy the current directory where we've checked out our source onto an SRC directory on the Docker container, which will serve as our build route point. Then, we will `pip install` the requirements, which is going to bring in TensorFlow and Keras connections, as well as the `h5` Python library that we'll use to save our model:

```
#packages needed by our server
RUN pip install -r /src/requirements.txt
```

Packages needed by our server

Here's the part that's different: we're actually going to train our model as part of our Docker build file, and this will create a model, train it, and save it. However, it'll be saving it to the Docker container, so that when we've built the Docker container image, or when we distribute it or use it elsewhere, that trained file will go with it. Finally, we have our `run` command to run our REST service, which will take advantage of the trained model file that's stored in the Docker image:

```
#packages needed by our server
RUN pip install -r /src/requirements.txt

#train the machine learning model
RUN cd /src && python train_mnist.py

#serve up a jupyter notebook
USER keras
WORKDIR /src
EXPOSE 5000
CMD cd /src && FLASK_ENV=development python server.py
```

Run our REST service

Now, we're going to build our container; we're using the `docker build` command, and again, using `-t` to tag it in `kerasvideo-server`. `.` means that we're running with the Dockerfile in the current directory:

```
test@test:~/Desktop/11519/kerasvideo-server-2018$ docker build -t kerasvideo-ser
ver-2018 .
```

The docker build command

On my system, this takes quite a while. Training it with the CPU took roughly 30 minutes to finish. This will vary based on the performance of your computer or whether or not you enabled GPU support. At the end of this, we'll have a Docker container that's ready to run so that we can use it as our REST server environment:

```
incarnation: 4282771416913401088
]
Downloading data from https://s3.amazonaws.com/img-datasets/mnist.npz
11476992/11490434 [============================>.] - ETA: 0s
Layer (type)                 Output Shape              Param #
=================================================================
conv2d_1 (Conv2D)            (None, 26, 26, 32)        320
_____
conv2d_2 (Conv2D)            (None, 24, 24, 64)        18496
_____
max_pooling2d_1 (MaxPooling2 (None, 12, 12, 64)        0
_____
dropout_1 (Dropout)          (None, 12, 12, 64)        0
_____
flatten_1 (Flatten)          (None, 9216)              0
_____
dense_1 (Dense)              (None, 128)               1179776
_____
dropout_2 (Dropout)          (None, 128)               0
_____
dense_2 (Dense)              (None, 10)                1290
=================================================================
Total params: 1,199,882
Trainable params: 1,199,882
Non-trainable params: 0
_____
None
Train on 60000 samples, validate on 10000 samples
Epoch 1/8
60000/60000 [==============================] - 168s - loss: 0.2092 - acc: 0.9357 - val_loss: 0.0462 - val_acc: 0.9853
Epoch 2/8
60000/60000 [==============================] - 167s - loss: 0.0790 - acc: 0.9767 - val_loss: 0.0358 - val_acc: 0.9885
Epoch 3/8
60000/60000 [==============================] - 167s - loss: 0.0611 - acc: 0.9811 - val_loss: 0.0321 - val_acc: 0.9901
Epoch 4/8
60000/60000 [==============================] - 167s - loss: 0.0499 - acc: 0.9847 - val_loss: 0.0297 - val_acc: 0.9899
Epoch 5/8
60000/60000 [==============================] - 173s - loss: 0.0410 - acc: 0.9870 - val_loss: 0.0327 - val_acc: 0.9900
Epoch 6/8
60000/60000 [==============================] - 167s - loss: 0.0385 - acc: 0.9882 - val_loss: 0.0276 - val_acc: 0.9916
Epoch 7/8
60000/60000 [==============================] - 167s - loss: 0.0318 - acc: 0.9899 - val_loss: 0.0313 - val_acc: 0.9902
Epoch 8/8
60000/60000 [==============================] - 166s - loss: 0.0295 - acc: 0.9907 - val_loss: 0.0267 - val_acc: 0.9913Using TensorFlow backend.
```

Docker container

Now that we have a built Docker container with a trained model and a REST service on it, we're going to run this service in order to make predictions.

Making predictions

In the previous section, we set up our Docker container, and now, in this section, we'll be using our Docker container to run a REST server and make predictions. We're going to be running our Docker container that we just created and then look at the connected built-in user interface to test our REST service. Finally, we'll post an image with that REST service so that we can see a prediction come back. We'll also see how you can call through to your service with curl, a command-line program that can post files.

Now, we're going to be starting up our Docker container. We'll be mapping the local port 5000 through to the container port 5000, which is the default in our REST service. Then, we'll start the service up. The `kerasvideo-server` container is the one we just created, and this container will take a second to start up and import TensorFlow. Then, we will load the model and serve it off of the local IP address on port 5000:

```
C:\11519\kerasvideo-server-master>docker run -p 5000:5000 kerasvideo-server-master
2018-07-25 06:07:07.197047: W tensorflow/core/platform/cpu_feature_guard.cc:45] The TensorFlow library wasn't compiled to use SSE4.1 instructions, but these
are available on your machine and could speed up CPU computations.
2018-07-25 06:07:07.197093: W tensorflow/core/platform/cpu_feature_guard.cc:45] The TensorFlow library wasn't compiled to use SSE4.2 instructions, but these
are available on your machine and could speed up CPU computations.
2018-07-25 06:07:07.197116: W tensorflow/core/platform/cpu_feature_guard.cc:45] The TensorFlow library wasn't compiled to use AVX instructions, but these are
 available on your machine and could speed up CPU computations.
2018-07-25 06:07:07.197121: W tensorflow/core/platform/cpu_feature_guard.cc:45] The TensorFlow library wasn't compiled to use AVX2 instructions, but these ar
e available on your machine and could speed up CPU computations.
2018-07-25 06:07:07.197125: W tensorflow/core/platform/cpu_feature_guard.cc:45] The TensorFlow library wasn't compiled to use FMA instructions, but these are
 available on your machine and could speed up CPU computations.

Layer (type)                 Output Shape              Param #
=================================================================
conv2d_1 (Conv2D)            (None, 26, 26, 32)        320
_____
conv2d_2 (Conv2D)            (None, 24, 24, 64)        18496
_____
max_pooling2d_1 (MaxPooling2 (None, 12, 12, 64)        0
_____
dropout_1 (Dropout)          (None, 12, 12, 64)        0
_____
flatten_1 (Flatten)          (None, 9216)              0
_____
dense_1 (Dense)              (None, 128)               1179776
_____
dropout_2 (Dropout)          (None, 128)               0
_____
dense_2 (Dense)              (None, 10)                1290
=================================================================
Total params: 1,199,882
Trainable params: 1,199,882
Non-trainable params: 0
_____
None
 * Serving Flask app "server" (lazy loading)
 * Environment: production
   WARNING: Do not use the development server in a production environment.
   Use a production WSGI server instead.
 * Debug mode: off
Using TensorFlow backend.
 * Running on http://0.0.0.0:5000/ (Press CTRL+C to quit)
```

Loading of the model

So, we open up localhost `5000/ui` in our browser, and we get a user interface that's been automatically generated by connection that documents the Swagger API:

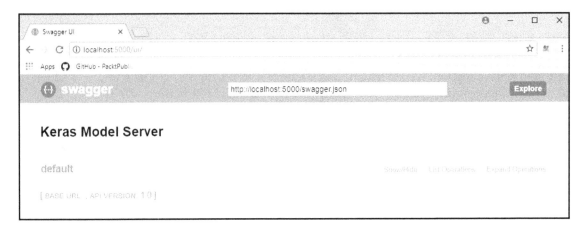

User interface

You can see the endpoint that we have created (`mnist/classify`), and you can just click on it and expand it so that you can look at our implementation notes, description, the parameters, the response type, and our file upload:

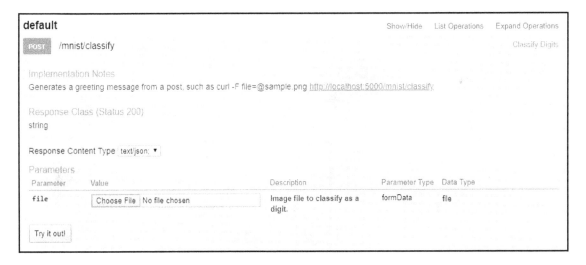

Explore the default option

Then, we'll go ahead and grab a `sample` digit that I had stored on disk, and we will post this through to our API with the **Try it out!** button in the lower left-hand corner. This will actually run our API for us. This shows the equivalent `curl` command from the command line that we'll be using here, as well as the **Request URL**. Here's our answer coming back from the **Response Body**, which correctly classifies this digit as a `0`:

```
Curl

curl -X POST --header 'Content-Type: multipart/form-data' --header 'Accept: text/json' {"type":"formData"} 'http://localhost:5000/

Request URL

http://localhost:5000/mnist/classify

Response Body

  {"digit": 0}

Response Code

200

Response Headers

{
  "date": "Sun, 03 Sep 2017 19:36:42 GMT",
  "server": "Werkzeug/0.12.2 Python/3.6.1",
  "content-length": "12",
  "content-type": "text/json;; charset=utf-8"
}
```

Final output (Response Body)

Now, let's try this from the command line. From the command line, this is a relatively straightforward operation. We're actually just going to use `curl` from the UNIX command prompt, and `-F` for form data posting. We have `file=` and here's the trick that `@` variable name and so it's `@var/data/sample.png`, which is our sample image. Then, we'll go ahead and pass that through to the URL, which is our service, and we will see that it correctly classifies:

```
$ curl -F file=@var/data/sample.png http://localhost:5000/mnist/classify
```

Using of curl command

Now, you've got to remember that the `file=` is the parameter name that matches up to what we created in our API definition YAML for Swagger, and that the multipart form data is how we're posting and uploading the image. So, with this basic kind of technique, you can use `curl`, or you can use other client libraries that you would use, say, from the web browser, in order to integrate your machine learning service into the rest of your application.

Summary

We've actually used a Swagger API definition to create a REST API model that then declaratively generates the Python framework in order for us to serve that API. We just had to put in a very small amount of code in order to get it running. Then, we created a Docker container that captures not only our running code that is our service, but our pre-trained machine learning model, which then forms a package so that we are able to deploy and use our container. Finally, we used this container in order to serve and make predictions.

Other Books You May Enjoy

If you enjoyed this book, you may be interested in these other books by Packt:

Deep Learning with TensorFlow - Second Edition
Giancarlo Zaccone, Md. Rezaul Karim

ISBN: 9781788831109

- Apply deep machine intelligence and GPU computing with TensorFlow
- Access public datasets and use TensorFlow to load, process, and transform the data
- Discover how to use the high-level TensorFlow API to build more powerful applications
- Use deep learning for scalable object detection and mobile computing
- Train machines quickly to learn from data by exploring reinforcement learning techniques
- Explore active areas of deep learning research and applications

TensorFlow 1.x Deep Learning Cookbook
Antonio Gulli, Amita Kapoor

ISBN: 9781788293594

- Install TensorFlow and use it for CPU and GPU operations
- Implement DNNs and apply them to solve different AI-driven problems.
- Leverage different data sets such as MNIST, CIFAR-10, and Youtube8m with TensorFlow and learn how to access and use them in your code.
- Use TensorBoard to understand neural network architectures, optimize the learning process, and peek inside the neural network black box.
- Use different regression techniques for prediction and classification problems
- Build single and multilayer perceptrons in TensorFlow
- Implement CNN and RNN in TensorFlow, and use it to solve real-world use cases.
- Learn how restricted Boltzmann Machines can be used to recommend movies.
- Understand the implementation of Autoencoders and deep belief networks, and use them for emotion detection.
- Master the different reinforcement learning methods to implement game playing agents.
- GANs and their implementation using TensorFlow.

Leave a review - let other readers know what you think

Please share your thoughts on this book with others by leaving a review on the site that you bought it from. If you purchased the book from Amazon, please leave us an honest review on this book's Amazon page. This is vital so that other potential readers can see and use your unbiased opinion to make purchasing decisions, we can understand what our customers think about our products, and our authors can see your feedback on the title that they have worked with Packt to create. It will only take a few minutes of your time, but is valuable to other potential customers, our authors, and Packt. Thank you!

Index

www.ingramcontent.com/pod-product-compliance
Lightning Source LLC
Chambersburg PA
CBHW080541060326
40690CB00022B/5200